VENEER or RE

THE QUESTION FOR C

Books by David H.J.Gay referred to in this volume:

A Case of Mistaken Identity: A Critique of Timothy Keller on Regeneration.

Assurance in the New Covenant.

Attracting Unbelievers to Church: Points to Ponder.

Battle for the Church: 1517-1644.

Christ Is All: No Sanctification by the Law.

Conversion Ruined: The New Perspective and the Conversion of Sinners.

Evangelicals Warned: Isaiah 30 Speaks Today.

False Brothers: Paul and Today.

Fivefold Sanctification.

Four 'Antinomians' Tried and Vindicated: Tobias Crisp, William Dell, John Eaton and John Saltmarsh.

In Church or In Christ?

Infant Baptism Tested.

Positional Sanctification: Two Consequences.

Priesthood: Our Need, God's Provision.

Public Worship: God-Ordained or Man-Invented?

Royal Reflections.

Sabbath Notes & Extracts.

Sabbath Questions: An open letter to Iain Murray.

Sowed Much, Reaped Little: Why?: The Sermon: The Gap between the Claim and the Result.

The Essential Sabbath.

The Hinge in Romans 1 – 8: A critique of N.T.Wright's view of Baptism and Conversion.

The Pastor: Does He Exist?

The Secret Stifler: Incipient Sandemanianism and Preaching the Gospel to Sinners.

Relationship Evangelism Exposed: A Blight on the Churches and the Ungodly.

Veneer or Reality?

The Question for Christendom

The kingdom of God does not consist in talk but in power.
1 Corinthians 4:20

...having the appearance [or form] of godliness, but denying its power.
2 Timothy 3:5

David H.J.Gay

BRACHUS

BRACHUS 2023

Scripture quotations come from a variety of versions

Hypocrites... love to stand and pray in the synagogues and at the street corners, that they may be seen by others. Truly, I say to you, they have received their reward.

Matthew 6:5

Scribes and... Pharisees... do all their deeds to be seen by others...Woe to you, scribes and Pharisees, hypocrites! For you clean the outside of the cup and the plate, but inside they are full of greed and self-indulgence. You blind Pharisee! First clean the inside of the cup and the plate, that the outside also may be clean. Woe to you, scribes and Pharisees, hypocrites! For you are like whitewashed tombs, which outwardly appear beautiful, but within are full of dead people's bones and all uncleanness. So you also outwardly appear righteous to others, but within you are full of hypocrisy and lawlessness.

Matthew 23:2-5,25-28

No one is a Jew who is merely one outwardly, nor is circumcision outward and physical. But a Jew is one inwardly, and circumcision is a matter of the heart, by the Spirit, not by the letter. His praise is not from man but from God.

Romans 2:28-29

These are waterless springs.

2 Peter 2:17

These are... waterless clouds.

Jude 12

You have the reputation of being alive, but you are dead.

Revelation 3:1

Appearances are deceiving.

Aesop

Never since the Lord Jesus Christ left the earth, was there so much formality and false profession as there is at the present day.

J.C.Ryle (1878)

Look at the church of the present day... 'Having a form of godliness but denying the power thereof'. It is the sin of the age – the sin which is ruining the churches of our land.

C.H.Spurgeon (1889)

Lord, make us as good as other people think we are.

Harry Matthews (*circa.* 1970)

Contents

APPENDICES

Introduction

By publishing this book, I hope to draw attention to the way in which two aspects of contemporary culture – namely, talk (or chat) and image – affect Christendom in general, and professing believers in particular.[1] Affect? Chat and image have played havoc with – and are increasingly playing havoc with – true spirituality, with the result that, for a growing number, profession of Christ amounts to little more than a veneer, a matter of chat and image. Such is my reading of much of contemporary church life. Hence my title: *Veneer or Reality? The Question for Christendom.*

---

[1] See my *The Pastor*; *Infant*; *Battle*; Appendix 2 'Christendom' in my *Relationship*. See my 'Not Talk But Power' and 'Reality Not Image' on my sermonaudio.com page.

Chat

Switch on your TV or radio, and you're almost bound to pick up a chat show. Media-chat is one of the preoccupations of the age. Professional chatterers make a living out of the eye-watering fees they receive for their willingness, at the drop of a hat, to chat on air – or television – about anything or nothing, and a vast number of men and women seem to enjoy listening to – or watching – the chattering class doing what they love to do; namely, chat, endlessly chat. Modern man, it seems, simply cannot get enough chat. And is willing to pay for it.

It is solemnly announced that the King or Prime Minister is suffering from bunions. The bigwigs at the BBC immediately spring into action, pulling out all the stops to set up an hour-long emergency programme, that very evening, amassing, at great expense, four 'experts' and a chairman who will let them – who will encourage them to – witter on about the constitutional and political consequences of bunions, not forgetting the medical and genetic aspects of the *hallux valgus*, and prognosticate about coming events – all because of those wretched deformities of the joints of the big toes. Chat is big business – and lucrative, to boot! It is one of the major opiate-diversions for the masses today.

Of course, the ability to chat – and the love of it – is as old as Adam. Going back not quite as far as that, a hundred years ago, when the *prima donna* orator of the time – David Lloyd-George – was asked what notice he would require if invited to make a speech, he replied to the effect that if he were to be restricted to a five-minute address, he would need a fortnight,[1] for a quarter of an hour, a week, but if he could speak without limit, he'd start now. He could chat, you see; he was never stuck for a word. Just fire the starting gun!

---

[1] That is, two weeks.

Lloyd-George illustrates another feature of chat. During the First World War, he knew how to move his audience when addressing a crowd from a public platform in order to get the nation to send its sons the Front. Very moving he was, too, and successful, but, alas, behind the scenes, he was equally adroit at keeping his own son clear of danger.

So much for chat – for now!

Image

Year in, year out, countless thousands of men and women spend a small fortune flying across the globe to visit Paris in order to join a queue to be allowed, a group at a time, to enter a room to catch a glimpse of the most famous painting in the world, the *Mona Lisa* by Leonardo da Vinci. This painting has been described as 'the best known, the most visited, the most written about, the most sung about, the most parodied work of art in the world'.[1] And for a few minutes, those who have laid out a great deal of money, and have gone to so much trouble and personal inconvenience, are allowed into the room where they may feast their eyes on the masterpiece.

But, the strange thing is, hardly any of them actually look at the painting when they get the chance. Certainly, they do not really look at it. Rather, they busy themselves taking out their smart phones, raising them over the heads of their fellow-rubber-necks in front of them, and gaze at the painting through the back of the said phones. Standing back and watching, it's like a swaying hedgehog with raised spines. What is more, the people don't actually look at the painting through their phone; their real purpose is to capture a digital image of the *Mona Lisa* on their phone. The fact that they could have obtained a better image at trivial cost and staying at home never enters their heads. Anyway that's not the point. It's not the painting, nor is it the image of the painting that matters. What the people long for – what they need – what they will spend and travel for is proof that they have actually been in the same room as the painting. They want an image of the painting on their phone, an image which they have captured for themselves.

---

[1] Wikipedia.

21

But that's not the end of it. Most of those who get into the Louvre, have another purpose: the real purpose of their visit is that they might actually turn their back of the painting and take a selfie – capturing an image of themselves with the *Mona Lisa* painting in the background.

Think about it! It's not the lady herself – Lisa Gherardini – that counts; it's not da Vinci's actual brushwork that counts; it's not the image of the painting that counts; what really matters is the image of self – me – in the same room as the *Mona Lisa*. Think! The reality was this noblewoman. Leonardo da Vinci painted an image of her, and a smart phone captures an image of that image. And the selfie captures an image of self with an image of that image of the Italian woman in the background. So what is the reality – the noblewoman, the image of the woman, the image of the image, or what? As the pigs and the men morphed into each other in George Orwell's *Animal Farm*, image and reality have changed place – or become one and the same. Image has become reality; and *vice-versa*.

We still have not exhausted the purpose of the *Mona Lisa* performance. By means of social media and internet availability, these countless selfie images are transmitted to millions within seconds. And that's the real purpose: take a selfie of me with my back to the *Mona Lisa*, and *post it on social media, craving as many 'likes' as I can get*. That's what it is all about!

It's not just the *Mona Lisa*. People use their phones to capture an image of the food they have cooked or paid good money for. Why? In order to post it on the internet. It's not the food that counts; it's the image of the food. Or rather, the publication of that image. *And the 'likes'.*

The world is awash with image (and 'likes'). And image is the thing – in all walks of life. Take politics. As I was beginning to write this in 2022, the Conservative party in the UK was choosing its new leader. Although typical Tory-party members remain more attuned to the printed word than the internet, the candidates realised that the image of themselves they project on social media platforms is still vital.[2] And surely we have not forgotten the way Donald Trump, as President, used – or, rather, abused – social media to conduct USA politics, including international 'diplomacy'.

Moreover, since computer software such as Photoshop (and even more sophisticated packages) are readily available to a mass market, we now know that the internet and the press is weighed down, not merely with image, but with *fake* image. So much so, people are rightly beginning to doubt what they see in the media. (The same goes for fake-news, both written and spoken).

The logical outcome is inevitable: sensible people will come to believe nothing is what it seems. In an age increasingly dominated by social media, we find ourselves living in a world of fantasy, in a culture dominated by image. It's not just the amateurs at the Louvre, or cooks sitting at their kitchen tables. I have mentioned politicians. The fact is, professional image-makers have set up dream-factories manufacturing fantasy worlds for us all to dwell in. Real life is a movie, and the movie is real life. The age in which we live might well be styled 'the age of the image': more images are produced in seconds today than were produced throughout the entire twentieth century. Global business managers, advertisers, bank governors, politicians, television producers, internet scammers, and the like, know that image and presentation is the key; vast sums of money can be made by clever use of image.[3]

---

[2] See 'Liz Truss v Rishi Sunak: Who's winning the social media war?' (BBC News website 23rd July 2022).
[3] A scammer who wants victims to move large sums of money into his account in a get-rich-quick scheme will present an image of affluence: he will been seen with an expensive car, watch, clothes, all in luxurious or exotic surroundings. And when he posts – if he ever does – any warning, he makes sure that the viewer's eyes are diverted by posting a catchy video alongside at the same time.

News, especially disaster, is now a spectacle and *vice-versa*. When mass television first erupted in the UK in the 50s, the set standing in the corner was dismissed by the smug, self-righteous, superior sophisticates as 'the goggle box in the room'. But joke has become reality. Most of us have succumbed. Marx got it wrong, at least for our time: goggling is now the people's opiate. A road accident on the north-bound motorway produces accidents on the south-bound because drivers continue to drive even though they are transfixed, goggling across the safety barrier.

Of course, this is nothing new; it's only the technology that's new. The careful cultivation of image has been with is since Adam fell. Fifty years ago, as I myself observed, alongside a viewing platform within sight of the Eiffel Tower, motor coaches would pull up in a constant stream, jam-packed with Japanese tourists, and out would pour streams of chattering men and women clutching cameras, collapsible tripods, light meters, flash guns, and all the rest of the paraphernalia required in those antediluvian days, the remainder of the gear swinging round their necks. Click, click, click went the shutters. Then a super-rapid packing up and scrabble back into coach to tear off into the traffic, heading for the next site – victim, I almost said – on the list. The whole process had taken little more time than it takes to read about it. The tourists who had travelled 6000 miles to see the Eiffel Tower had not actually – really – seen the massive wrought-iron construction. They had captured an image of the Eiffel Tower. Which, of course, is what they wanted. Today, it would be a smart-phone selfie posted on the worldwide web, going viral while-you-wait. Or, at least, that would be the hope.

Advertisers no longer try to sell a product; they have long learned better! A product? What's that? They sell a dream; they persuade customers to spend to buy into a dream conjured up by an image; as the 1997 pop song expressed it:

'Live the Dream'![4] Presentation, show, appearance, image, parade, packaging, display, fantasy, aspiration, the promise of the holy grail of happiness, contentment, fulfilment, satisfaction... you name it. My dentist, to judge by the permanent writing on the wall behind the receptionist's desk, is in the business of selling me the smile I deserve; that is, the image I am supposed to crave.

As I have said, I don't want to give the impression that all this is a modern problem.

Form, or show, outward appearance, image, as I have hinted, has been top of the agenda since Adam. The Nazi, Joseph Goebbels, was a past master at the game on behalf of his god, Adolf Hitler.[5] Read the novels of Jane Austen, and you will come across a society dominated by form, appearance, manners, etiquette, image, how things look. Her novels not only poke withering fun at those whose lives were consumed by such, but their story-lines depend absolutely on it. Victorian society, similarly, was consumed with outward appearance, with image: what went on behind closed doors often bore little resemblance to outward appearance.[6] But it

---

[4] 'I just want to be thinking thoughts that I think,/ Dreaming my dreams and drifting within./ I don't know where I'm goin,/ But I know where I've been./ Come on, live your dream'.

[5] When seeking power, Hitler could project an image a man of law and democracy, one who was decent and honourable, and when he got his hands on absolute power, he projected an image of a Reich ruled by order, work and discipline. But it was all an illusion. He used democracy only to overthrow it, and his chaotic government of the country was a system – if it can be dignified by calling it such – amounting to nothing more than an anthill of innuendo, intrigue, sycophantism, confusion, rivalry, betrayal and social-Darwinianism. Hitler himself was indolent.

[6] Indeed, Albert and Victoria were determined to rescue the disastrous Hanoverian monarchy in a time of republican revolution by presenting the royal family as a model of domestic bliss and moral purity. On the first count, the mother (in particular) and her nine children proved a disastrous failure, and on the second, the loucheness of some of Victoria's offspring remains a byword, But

Image

was the outward that was vital – how things looked; the inward, the real, could, by and large, take care of itself – or, not!

A euphemism for 'propaganda' in these PC days, of course, is 'presentation'. Who doesn't realise that presentation is king? When, in 1996, the would-be Labour Prime Minister, Tony Blair, repeated the mantra: 'Education! Education! Education!', what he really meant – what really happened when he seeking to get his hands on power – was 'Presentation! Presentation! Presentation!' Don't take my word for it. Roy Hattersley (and he should know) spoke of the way New Labour under Blair ditched the embarrassing (for electoral purposes) Clause IV of the 1918 Labour party manifesto (that is, workers had to get their hands on all the levers of power).[7] In 1995, there was a brief discussion on the principle (cleverly managed and conducted at a time to minimise debate) until, as Hattersley cynically put it, the debate was 'disposed of before coffee time', after which, 'we were able to turn to the aspects of policy we most enjoyed – not formulation but presentation'.[8] Hattersley remarked on

---

the monarchy survived – just – to be fully rescued by Edward VII, Victoria's heir, who turned his parents' model on its head: outward show and ceremonial, not domestic fidelity, was key for him. The principle worked, and by it the monarchy has remained intact (just about) to this day: outward form is what counts, despite what goes on behind (mostly) closed doors. In a fallen world, among natural men, it always does; the institutional Church has not escaped – the charade, in the UK, being enforced by the connection between the Monarch and the State Church. See my 'Tale of Two Coronations: Farcical & Real' on my sermonaudio.com web page, and also in my *Royal Reflections.*

[7] 'To secure for the workers by hand or by brain the full fruits of their industry and the most equitable distribution thereof that may be possible upon the basis of the common ownership of the means of production, distribution and exchange, and the best obtainable system of popular administration and control of each industry or service'.

[8] Roy Hattersley: *Who Goes Home? Scenes from a Political Life,* Little, Brown and Company, London, 1995, p292.

Image

Peter Mandelson's brilliance in engineering all this, but did not fail to draw attention to the calamitous downside:

> Image often took precedence over the ideas, and presentation, instead of being no more than a delivery system, was regarded as the mighty warhead which would blow the enemy to pieces.[9]

So much for image – for now!

---

[9] Hattersley p293. There was no shortage in the number of examples he gave to illustrate what he was talking about. Here's another that came after Hattersley's book: think about the wrapping that sold the 2003 Iraq War to the citizens of the UK.

The Point: Evangelical Christendom

Chat and image, I submit, are two of the chief preoccupations of our time. In this book, I am concerned with both – but not in society, TV, business, politics, and the like. Oh no! Nothing better can be expected from the world. Believers are living in a fallen society, a fallen world made up of fallen, sinful men and women, a wicked world, a world under Satanic domination:

> All, both Jews and Greeks, are under sin, as it is written: 'None is righteous, no, not one; no one understands; no one seeks for God. All have turned aside; together they have become worthless; no one does good, not even one... There is no fear of God before their eyes'... There is no distinction: for all have sinned and fall short of the glory of God (Rom. 3:9-23).

Believers know that:

> ...the god of this world has blinded the minds of the unbelievers (2 Cor. 4:4).

Nobody can doubt the enslaving power which sin has – in all its forms. Christ laid it on the line when addressing the Jews – a religious people if ever there was one:

> The truth will set you free... Truly, truly, I say to you, everyone who practices sin is a slave to sin (John. 8:32-34).

Indeed, believers know that they themselves were once held in this ruinous captivity, this slavery to sin:

> You were dead in the trespasses and sins in which you once walked, following the course of this world, following the prince of the power of the air, the spirit that is now at work in the sons of disobedience – among whom we all once lived in the passions of our flesh, carrying out the desires of the body and the mind, and were by nature children of wrath, like the rest of mankind (Eph. 2:1-3).

But that:

The Lord Jesus Christ... gave himself for our sins to deliver us from the present evil age (Gal. 1:3-4).

We know that we [true believers] are from God, and the whole world lies in the power of the evil one (1 John 5:19; see also John 12:31; 17:15).

As Christ, still addressing the Jews, declared:

If the Son sets you free, you will be free indeed (John 8:36).

The point is, preoccupation with chat and form is a mark of fallen man. It takes a signal demonstration of God's power to put a stop to chat, to silence unbelievers, 'that every mouth may be stopped' (Rom. 3:19).

Yes, this age is evil, and the world is ruled by Satan. No wonder, then, that chat and appearance, talk and image, show and form, dominates such a world. Look how Adam and Eve, as soon as they fell, were instinctively consumed with appearance, fig leaves and talk, making excuses, passing the buck (Gen. 3:7-13). Whatever else was going through their minds, they weren't stuck for words, words to put themselves in the best light. And ever since, all of Adam's descendents have been born with the same innate love of chat and form, the ability to come up with reasons to chat to enable them to fulfil their *desire* to chat.

But it is not what is going on in the world that interests me; it is what is going on in the churches, among believers; that is what concerns me. Church trend-setters – evangelicals in the van – have cottoned on to what makes the world tick, what it likes. And that is chat and image.[1] Why not go some way to meeting the world's aspirations, baiting the hook, to engineer[2] the chance to evangelise them? Evangelical trend-setters have spotted what works in the world. Why shouldn't

---

[1] On image, see my *A Case*.

[2] A seemingly in-word for the evangelical trend-setters today. See my *Relationship*.

that which works in the world not work in the church? By unearthing what works in the world, and then devising sophisticated schemes and programmes based on these successful models, the clever opinion-formers have enabled failing churches to 're-engineer' (here we go again!) themselves in order to bring 'success'. Image and presentation, these trend-setters know, are key to this 're-engineering'. The 'failing' in question is falling church attendance; 'success', naturally, is increasing church attendance.

And it works; this 're-engineering' of the *ekklēsia* is in many cases leading to a rising church-attendance. Of course some churches can't or won't keep up, get trampled in the lemming-like rush, and peter out. But no matter; the few remaining attendees can always switch from the defunct, dying corner-shop to the big, successful superstore down the road. This, in turn, ensures the further success of the successful in boosting church attendance. The stick-in-the-mud-church withers, while the modern dream-factory flourishes like a green bay tree planted by a never-failing stream.

In all this, image and chat are king – in the world and in the church. It is the age of image and chat. It is presentation – image – that attracts the consumers. But that's only the start of it. Once the consumers have been attracted, the church knows it must teach them how to chat; that is, teach them to use the right language. And project the right image. Evangelical Christendom has done its homework, and done it well; it has mastered the lessons it has gleaned from the world: having the right image and using the right chat is what spells success. Moreover, it has set up polished courses for the 'not-yet-converted' to teach them – in the spirit of N.T.Wright[3] – to learn 'their part in the play', and ham it for all its worth!

---

[3] See my *Conversion*; *Hinge*.

I have already said that although this has mushroomed in the present generation, and is 'flourishing' – what an oxymoron – it is not only a modern phenomenon. Let me now make good that claim.

A Glance at History

As already noted, dependence on image and chat began with Adam and Eve – it erupted immediately following their fall; when confronted by God, they instinctively turned to it. With the passing of the centuries, these instinctive preoccupations have never lost their power to charm fallen man, especially in his relationship to God. Although it is the way in which this plays out in contemporary evangelical Christendom that concerns me, I need to take a glance at history. We, today, are living out our particular section of history, but we are not living in isolation. We are, all of us, deeply, inevitably, affected by what has gone before. And we will be somewhat impoverished if we do not have some understanding of what that past is and how it plays into our experience today.

Consequently, I need to expose the part image and chat played in the life of Israel, both in the days before Christ and during his lifetime. Then I need to look at the influence of image and chat in the apostolic churches; then I want briefly to trace how this approach has affected church history through the centuries; and so to us today.

Image and chat in Israel

Israel always had a problem with image. The old covenant was a time of religious spectacle – tabernacle, temple, sacrifices, incense, gold, trumpets, vestments, and so on, colours, sounds and smells.[1] In the memorable words of David, (as recorded in KJV or AV): 'The house that is to be builded for the LORD must be exceeding magnifical, of

---

[1] The medieval Church, which (see below) was based on the old covenant, not the new, gives us a clear sense of what it must have been like. The coronation of Charles III on 6th May 2023 displayed to millions the sort of glossy but diabolical pageant and pantomime which Christendom can produce. Even so, though it aped it, it still failed to rise in glitz to the coronation of a pope.

fame and of glory throughout all countries' (1 Chron. 22:5; see also 2 Chron. 2:9; 6:2). 'Exceeding magnifical'! And in that 'house' (some house!), certain spectacular rituals had constantly to be gone through. So much of the old covenant was external: how tempting it was, how easy it was, therefore, for the children of Israel to concentrate on the external and forget the internal. They could simply turn up, watch (as much as they were allowed), smell and listen, open-mouthed.

Take the building, whether tabernacle or temple; if the building was right, all was right? No! God, in the days of both Moses and Solomon, gave the Israelites clear instruction about its inadequacy. The former completed the building of the tabernacle; the latter, the temple. In both cases, all was fitted out precisely as God had instructed. Very good! But the form, the shell, the outward – even in the days of the old covenant – was not enough, even though it had been constructed exactly as God had commanded (Ex. 25:9,40; Num. 8:4; Acts 7:44; Heb. 8:5); the presence and power of God was essential. And that is just what God made clear to his people. After the tabernacle was complete, but was still just an empty form or shell:

> Then the cloud covered the tent of meeting, and the glory of the LORD filled the tabernacle. And Moses was not able to enter the tent of meeting because the cloud settled on it, and the glory of the LORD filled the tabernacle (Ex. 40:34-35).[2]

As for the temple, all was prepared, and then:

> The house, the house of the LORD, was filled with a cloud, so that the priests could not stand to minister because of the cloud, for the glory of the LORD filled the house of God (2 Chron. 5:13-14).

It should have been impossible for Israel to miss the lesson God was so plainly teaching them: the external form may be

---

[2] See my 'Obedience & Power' and 'Cloud, Fire, Glory!' on my sermonaudio.com web page.

pristine, but without the presence and power of God all was vain, worthless – and worse; it would simply encourage Israel's dependence on form and show. Just keep watching! Alas, for the overwhelming majority of Jews, ignoring the inward, the heart, the power, and the living experience and concentrating on the external, the show, the appearance, the shell, the image, was all that Judaism amounted to. As long as the veneer was intact, all was well.

It was not! Christ saw it in his day and he pulled no punches in condemning it:

> Hypocrites... love to stand and pray in the synagogues and at the street corners, that they may be seen by others. Truly, I say to you, they have received their reward... Scribes and... Pharisees... do all their deeds to be seen by others (Matt. 6:5; 23:2-5).

As for chat, Israel might use the right words, but here again, the presence and power of God in the heart was essential. God left his people in no doubt about it. He addressed his people through Isaiah, complaining:

> This people draw near with their mouth and honour me with their lips, while their hearts are far from me, and their fear of me is a commandment taught by men (Isa. 29:13).

And God warned Ezekiel not to be fooled by fine words:

> As for you, son of man, your people who talk together about you by the walls and at the doors of the houses, say to one another, each to his brother: 'Come, and hear what the word is that comes from the LORD'. And they come to you as people come, and they sit before you as my people, and they hear what you say but they will not do it; for with lustful talk in their mouths they act; their heart is set on their gain. And behold, you are to them like one who sings lustful songs with a beautiful voice and plays well on an instrument, for they hear what you say, but they will not do it. When this comes – and come it will! – then they will know that a prophet has been among them (Ezek. 33:30-33).

Christ could not have been more blunt:

35

Beware of practicing your righteousness before other people in order to be seen by them... When you give to the needy, sound no trumpet before you, as the hypocrites do in the synagogues and in the streets, that they may be praised by others... When you give to the needy, do not let your left hand know what your right hand is doing, so that your giving may be in secret... When you pray, you must not be like the hypocrites. For they love to stand and pray in the synagogues and at the street corners, that they may be seen by others... When you pray, do not heap up empty phrases as the Gentiles do, for they think that they will be heard for their many words... When you fast, do not look gloomy like the hypocrites, for they disfigure their faces that their fasting may be seen by others... When you fast, anoint your head and wash your face, that your fasting may not be seen by others... (Matt. 6:1-18).

You hypocrites! Well did Isaiah prophesy of you, when he said: 'This people honours me with their lips, but their heart is far from me; in vain do they worship me, teaching as doctrines the commandments of men' (Matt. 15:7-9).

Christ exposed the way the Jews glossed – and so circumvented – God's commandments by the things they said: 'You have a fine way of getting free of obedience [that is, avoiding obedience – DG]: God said... but you say' (see Mark 7:9-7). Chat, chat, chat and image.

So much for the old covenant and Israel.

What about the new covenant? What about the time of the apostles?

Image and chat in the days of the apostles

Paul, knowing that fallen man is ever the same, was outspoken on the issue:

No one is a Jew who is merely one outwardly, nor is circumcision outward and physical. But a Jew is one inwardly, and circumcision is a matter of the heart, by the Spirit, not by the letter. His praise is not from man but from God (Rom. 2:28-29).

36

This powerful assertion applied to Israel in the old covenant, of course, but its real significance for Paul was in his day, the here and now of the days of the new covenant. It applied to the people he could describe as 'the Israel of God' (Gal. 6:16).

'The Israel of God'. As the apostle said to the Galatians:

> Those of faith... are the sons of Abraham... Those who are of faith are blessed along with Abraham, the man of faith... If [since] you are Christ's, then you are Abraham's offspring, heirs according to promise (Gal. 3:7-9,29).

'The Israel of God'. As the apostle said to the Philippians:

> We are the circumcision, who worship by the Spirit of God and glory in Christ Jesus and put no confidence in the flesh (Phil. 3:3).

Peter, writing to believers, spelled out their standing before God:

> You are a chosen race, a royal priesthood, a holy nation, a people for his own possession, that you may proclaim the excellencies of him who called you out of darkness into his marvellous light. Once you were not a people, but now you are God's people; once you had not received mercy, but now you have received mercy (1 Pet. 2:9-10).

Clearly, then, Paul's words about 'a true Jew' apply to every professing believer:

> No one is a [real believer] who is merely one outwardly, nor is circumcision outward and physical. But a [real believer] is one inwardly, and circumcision is a matter of the heart, by the Spirit, not by the letter. His praise is not from man but from God (Rom. 2:28-29).

James too, spoke of the ever-present danger – the sin – of judging by appearance:

> My brothers, show no partiality as you hold the faith in our Lord Jesus Christ, the Lord of glory. For if a man wearing a gold ring and fine clothing comes into your assembly, and a poor man in shabby clothing also comes in, and if you pay

attention to the one who wears the fine clothing and say: 'You sit here in a good place', while you say to the poor man: 'You stand over there', or: 'Sit down at my feet', have you not then made distinctions among yourselves and become judges with evil thoughts? (Jas. 2:1-4).

And so to the two key verses:

The kingdom of God does not consist in talk [or chat] but in power (1 Cor. 4:20).

And, one of the marks of apostasy through this age, is that there will those:

...having the appearance [or form] of godliness, but denying its power (2 Tim. 3:5).

As for that last, since Paul told Timothy to 'avoid such people' (2 Tim. 3:5), we know the younger man had to face such at Ephesus. Peter and Jude used graphic illustrations, describing such professors as 'waterless springs' (2 Pet. 2:17) and 'waterless clouds' (Jude 12). What use are waterless springs and waterless clouds in drought – all appearance and no substance!

So much for apostolic times. What happened after the apostles?

Image and chat in the time of the Fathers

Following the death of the apostles, the Fathers went back to the old covenant (and paganism), and introduced priests, clergy/laity, titles, hierarchy, sacerdotalism, sacramentalism, sacred buildings, robes, and the like, into the life of the *ekklēsia*.[3] It was inevitable, therefore, that under such corrupt pressure, fallen man's obsession with image and chat should, as it had in Israel in the days of the old covenant, become

---

[3] See my *The Pastor*. See also 'Excursus on the Vestments of the Early Church', which may be found on the internet at biblestudytools.com/history/early-church-fathers/post-nicene/vol-14.

embedded in the new covenant. The combining of State and Church, politics united to religion – the invention of Christendom,[4] no less – enforced the innate love of image and chat among professed believers. The Dark Ages had begun!

How clearly image and chat were played out in the medieval papacy, which reduced spirituality to the performance of, and observation of, a gorgeous, priestly spectacle, enacted in a language that the overwhelming majority – including many of the actors themselves (that is, the priests) – did not understand.[5] This only added to the sense of mystery. But from start to finish it was a tragic farce.

As I have already noted, the coronation of Charles III on 6th May 2023 was a glaring example of this Christendom-theatre performance. And, of course, while it stemmed from the Fathers, it had been tinkered with by the Reformers.[6]

Image and chat in the time of the Reformers

The Reformers certainly tried to row back from the gaudy pantomime they inherited, and were largely successful in the area of soteriology. But, alas, as far as the *ekklēsia* was concerned, they simply replaced the activity of priests with the activity of preachers; image and chat still held sway. Instead of watching the priest in his 'holy vestments' parading (according to a set choreography) about 'the house of God', offering mass, the faithful now sat before a

---

[4] See my *The Pastor*; *Infant*; *Battle*; Appendix 2 'Christendom' in my *Relationship*.

[5] Hence the origin of the phrase *hocus pocus*, which almost certainly came from *hoc est corpus meum* (this is my body). In medieval times, this phrase largely became an incantation gabbled in dog-Latin by a priest who often did not understand it, half-heard by congregations who definitely did not understand it. As for the theology behind it...! Hence *hocus-pocus*.

[6] See my 'A Tale of Two Coronations: Farcical and True' on my sermonaudio.com web page. See also my *Royal*.

suitably-attired presbyter, in order, through eye and ear to absorb his preaching; in both cases, there was the ever-present risk that the many-headed might simply be watching and listening to a mere professional performance.[7] John Milton's 'large-writ priest'!

Image and chat in our time

Coming to our day – in the digital era, with countless 'church services' and sermons (video and audio) on tap, image, spectacle and chat have reached even dizzier heights. See my comments above, on the events of 6th May 2023.

Martin Luther, though he hated the Anabaptists, envied their *ekklēsia* life, and struggled to get something like it among his followers, but in vain; the only way to get it was to jettison Christendom! In their turn, the puritans tried desperately to turn image into reality among their followers. It proved an uphill struggle. Heavy doses of the old-covenant law was their prescription. But trying to legalise people into a conforming-obedience to the gospel is a far cry from regeneration, true conversion to Christ.[8] The only cure was precisely that which Paul spoke of; namely, the Spirit's power from start to finish. Nothing else will do.

Fundamentally, of course, it is the old story – the fall, sin. The devil has been playing the same game and pulling the strings since Eden. He pulled those strings in the first *ekklēsias*. And that is why Paul, moved by the Spirit, wrote against it.

Hence, let it never be forgotten:

> The kingdom of God does not consist in talk but in power (1 Cor. 4:20).

---

[7] On occasion, they could watch while he actually transferred a baby out of Adam into Christ by means of few drops of water and the repetition of the right mumbo jumbo! Or so the gullible believed – or, crossing fingers, hoped.

[8] See my *Christ*.

And we are to beware of:

> ...having the appearance [or form] of godliness, but denying its power (2 Tim. 3:5).

Getting to the Root: Power

One of the marks of apostasy throughout this age is that there will be those:

> ...having the appearance [or form] of godliness, but denying its power (2 Tim. 3:5).

And, as Paul categorically stated it:

> The kingdom of God does not consist in talk [or chat] but in power (1 Cor. 4:20).

Before we come to the particular, a look at the general.

In the profession of Christ, there are three things: 'appearance' (or form or image), 'talk' (or chat), and 'power'. We can have appearance or image, we can have talk, we can have both; but the great essential is power. The sober truth is that appearance and/or talk is no guarantee of power. But without power, we have nothing and we are nothing as far as the profession of Christ is concerned. We have the veneer, but not the reality; the varnish may shine, but it is only base metal or cheap wood.

Clearly, 'power' is a key new-covenant word. It has to be. Not only do we have these two verses, but, even more fundamentally, since we are in the age of the new covenant – the age of the Spirit – 'power' must be the word; spiritual power, that is. The presence and power of the Spirit is the hallmark of the new covenant, clearly distinguishing it from the old.[1]

John the Baptist's declaration:

> I baptise you with water for repentance, but he who is coming after me is mightier than I, whose sandals I am not worthy to carry. He will baptise you with the Holy Spirit and fire. His winnowing fork is in his hand, and he will

---

[1] See my 'Paul's Answer: The Spirit' in my *False.*

clear his threshing floor and gather his wheat into the barn,
but the chaff he will burn with unquenchable fire (Matt.
3:11-12; see also Mark 1:8; Luke 3:16; John 1:33).

Then we have Christ's assertion, and John's explanation.
First, Christ's declaration:

If anyone thirsts, let him come to me and drink. Whoever
believes in me, as the Scripture has said: 'Out of his heart
will flow rivers of living water'.

Then, John's explanation of this vital assertion:

Now this he said about the Spirit, whom those who believed
in him were to receive, for as yet the Spirit had not been
given, because Jesus was not yet glorified (John 7:37-39).

Again, Christ's promise:

I tell you the truth: it is to your advantage that I go away,
for if I do not go away, the Helper [that is, the Spirit] will
not come to you. But if I go, I will send him to you (John
16:7).

And the coming of the Spirit spelled power!

We have Christ's promise and command to his disciples
when he was preparing them for their work in the new age:

And Jesus came and said to them: 'All authority [or power]
in heaven and on earth has been given to me. Go therefore
and make disciples of all nations, baptising them in the
name of the Father and of the Son and of the Holy Spirit,
teaching them to observe all that I have commanded you.
And behold, I am with you always, to the end of the age'
(Matt. 28:18-20).

Go into all the world and proclaim the gospel to the whole
creation. Whoever believes and is baptised will be saved,
but whoever does not believe will be condemned (Mark.
16:15-16).

What a massive undertaking – worldwide evangelism –
something far beyond any human resource to accomplish! To
equip his disciples for it, Christ gave them his promise of
power:

Thus it is written, that the Christ should suffer and on the third day rise from the dead, and that repentance for the forgiveness of sins should be proclaimed in his name to all nations, beginning from Jerusalem. You are witnesses of these things. And behold, I am sending the promise of my Father upon you. But stay in the city until you are clothed with power from on high (Luke 24:47-49).

[Christ] ordered them not to depart from Jerusalem, but to wait for the promise of the Father, which, he said: 'You heard from me; for John baptised with water, but you will be baptised with the Holy Spirit not many days from now... You will receive power when the Holy Spirit has come upon you, and you will be my witnesses in Jerusalem and in all Judea and Samaria, and to the end of the earth' (Acts 1:4-8).

And it wasn't long before the Spirit descended upon them, immediately demonstrating his power in and among his people by the conversion of three thousand Jews under Peter's preaching that very same day (Acts 2).

And then there was the miraculous cure of the beggar at the Beautiful gate of the temple. Peter explained to the crowd which had gathered in amazement:

Men of Israel, why do you wonder at this, or why do you stare at us, as though by our own power or piety we have made him walk? (Acts 3:12).

And power was the chief anxiety of the Jewish authorities who felt threatened by what was happening: 'By what power or by what name did you do this?' they demanded of Peter and John. 'Then Peter, filled with the Holy Spirit, said to them':

Rulers of the people and elders, if we are being examined today concerning a good deed done to a crippled man, by what means this man has been healed, let it be known to all of you and to all the people of Israel that by the name of Jesus Christ of Nazareth, whom you crucified, whom God raised from the dead – by him this man is standing before you well.

In short:

> And with great power the apostles were giving their testimony to the resurrection of the Lord Jesus (Acts 4:7-10,33).

And they were not alone:

> Stephen, full of grace and power, was doing great wonders and signs among the people (Acts 6:8).

And so it went on until, in his letters, Paul set out the principles of 'power', the power that had been shown throughout the Acts in the preaching of the gospel, not least in his own preaching:

> Christ did not send me to baptise but to preach the gospel, and not with words of eloquent wisdom, lest the cross of Christ be emptied of its power... We preach Christ crucified, a stumbling block to Jews and folly to Gentiles, but to those who are called, both Jews and Greeks, Christ the power of God and the wisdom of God... I was with you in weakness and in fear and much trembling, and my speech and my message were not in plausible words of wisdom, but in demonstration of the Spirit and of power, so that your faith might not rest in the wisdom of men but in the power of God (1 Cor. 1:18,24; 2:3-5).

Again, when dealing with his opponents at Corinth, he majored on power:

> I will come to you soon, if the Lord wills, and I will find out not the talk of these arrogant people but their power. For the kingdom of God does not consist in talk but in power (1 Cor. 4:19-20).

> We put no obstacle in anyone's way, so that no fault may be found with our ministry, but as servants of God we commend ourselves in every way: by great endurance, in afflictions, hardships, calamities, beatings, imprisonments, riots, labours, sleepless nights, hunger; by purity, knowledge, patience, kindness, the Holy Spirit, genuine love; by truthful speech, and the power of God... (2 Cor. 6:3-10).

Writing to the Thessalonians, he said:

> We know, brothers loved by God, that he has chosen you,
> because our gospel came to you not only in word, but also
> in power and in the Holy Spirit and with full conviction (1
> Thess. 1:4-5).

And in his second letter to the Thessalonians he returned to
the subject of power:

> We always pray for you, that our God may make you
> worthy of his calling and may fulfil every resolve for good
> and every work of faith by his power, so that the name of
> our Lord Jesus may be glorified in you, and you in him,
> according to the grace of our God and the Lord Jesus Christ
> (2 Thess. 1:11-12).

To Timothy:

> God gave us a spirit not of fear but of power and love and
> self-control. Therefore do not be ashamed of the testimony
> about our Lord, nor of me his prisoner, but share in
> suffering for the gospel by the power of God (2 Tim. 1:7-8).

So much for the general principle. One of the leading marks
or characteristics of the new-covenant age is power. But
what, specifically, are we to understand by 'power' in the
two verses in question? Here they are again:

> ...having the appearance [or form] of godliness, but denying
> its power (2 Tim. 3:5).

And:

> The kingdom of God does not consist in talk but in power
> (1 Cor. 4:20).

Probing the meaning of 'power' – the great essential – in
these two verses will be the subject of the next chapter.
Because Paul has said far more about power in the
Corinthian letters than in his letters to Timothy, I regard the
Corinthian passage as key – and so I start with it.

The Power in Question

Here, again, is the key verse:

> The kingdom of God does not consist in talk but in power
> (1 Cor. 4:20).[1]

'Power' is a vital word in Paul's two letters to the Corinthians:

> Christ did not send me to baptise but to preach the gospel,
> and not with words of eloquent wisdom, lest the cross of
> Christ be emptied of its power... We preach Christ
> crucified, a stumbling block to Jews and folly to Gentiles,
> but to those who are called, both Jews and Greeks, Christ
> the power of God and the wisdom of God... I was with you
> in weakness and in fear and much trembling, and my
> speech and my message were not in plausible words of
> wisdom, but in demonstration of the Spirit and of power, so
> that your faith might not rest in the wisdom of men but in
> the power of God (1 Cor. 1:18,24; 2:3-5).

When dealing with his opponents at Corinth, the apostle majored on power:

> I will come to you soon, if the Lord wills, and I will find
> out not the talk of these arrogant people but their power.
> For the kingdom of God does not consist in talk but in
> power (1 Cor. 4:19-20).

When he was urging the Corinthians to discipline the incestuous brother, he reminded them of the power which Christ had bestowed on them as an *ekklēsia*:

> When you are assembled in the name of the Lord Jesus and
> my spirit is present, with the power of our Lord Jesus... (1
> Cor. 5:4).

And so it goes on:

---

[1] For more on this argument in this chapter, see 'Paul's Answer:
The Spirit' in my *False Brothers: Paul and Today*.

49

God raised the Lord and will also raise us up by his power (1 Cor. 6:14).

What then is my reward? That in my preaching I may present the gospel free of charge, so as not to make full use of my right [or power or authority] in the gospel (1 Cor. 9:18).

[The body] is sown in dishonour; it is raised in glory. It is sown in weakness; it is raised in power (1 Cor. 15:43).

Paul spoke of his 'ministry' by 'the power of God' (2 Cor. 6:7).

And of his own experience of how to deal with personal trouble in trial and affliction:

[Christ] said to me: 'My grace is sufficient for you, for my power is made perfect in weakness'. Therefore I will boast all the more gladly of my weaknesses, so that the power of Christ may rest upon me (2 Cor. 12:9).

Referring to his proposed visit to sort out the disorder at Corinth, the apostle said:

We... are weak in him, but in dealing with you we will live with him by the power of God... I write these things while I am away from you, that when I come I may not have to be severe in my use of the power that the Lord has given me for building up and not for tearing down (2 Cor. 13:4,10).

So much for 'power' in the first key verse. And now for the second verse:

...having the appearance [or form] of godliness, but denying its power (2 Tim. 3:5).

Paul could remind Timothy of:

...the gift of God, which is in you through the laying on of my hands, for God gave us a spirit not of fear but of power and love and self-control. Therefore do not be ashamed of the testimony about our Lord, nor of me his prisoner, but share in suffering for the gospel by the power of God (2 Tim. 1:6-8).

* * *

The questions for us are: What does this power consist of today? And where are we to find it? How do we get it? How does it show itself?

Let me follow the apostle's example and start with a few negatives. We have the apostle's clear statements:

> The kingdom of God does not consist in talk but in power (1 Cor. 4:20).

And:

> ...having the appearance [or form] of godliness, but denying its power (2 Tim. 3:5).

So far, so good: the key necessity in Christian experience is not talk, image or show, but power, inward spiritual power, power which only comes from the Spirit of God himself.

But as we have seen, in the early years of this age of the new covenant, the Spirit's power was displayed in preaching, and in miracles and signs. Even more fundamentally, it was displayed in regenerating, convicting and converting dead sinners to Christ, followed by a life-long increasing transformation of them into conformity into Christ's likeness – 'those whom [God] foreknew he also predestined to be conformed to the image of his Son, in order that he might be the firstborn among many brothers' (Rom. 8:29) – as they are 'walking by the Spirit', 'living by the Spirit' 'keeping in step with the Spirit' (Gal. 5:16,25). And that stood at the head of the list, coming first before all else: if sinners were not regenerated, convicted and converted, and had the energising power of the Spirit to live under Christ's law, they could engage in no preaching, take no meaningful part in any miracles.

The question, then, is not: Did the early *ekklēsia* have power in the sense that it had success in preaching, and displayed a range of spiritual, miraculous gifts? There is no doubt that it did. As for us today, some would say that the power referred to in the two key verses – that vital power – is exactly that. I do not agree. I am convinced that what the apostle was referring to – and what applies to us today, and is of the utmost importance – is the essential possession of the power of the Spirit in regeneration, conviction and conversion of sinners to Christ, with a life-long transformation of the converted into increasing conformity to Christ's likeness.

Christ's warning must not be forgotten:

> Not everyone who says to me: 'Lord, Lord', will enter the kingdom of heaven, but the one who does the will of my Father who is in heaven. On that day many will say to me: 'Lord, Lord, did we not prophesy in your name, and cast out demons in your name, and do many mighty works in your name?' And then will I declare to them: 'I never knew you; depart from me, you workers of lawlessness' (Matt. 7:21-23).

When the apostle told the Roman believers:

> Those who live according to the flesh set their minds on the things of the flesh, but those who live according to the Spirit set their minds on the things of the Spirit. For to set the mind on the flesh is death, but to set the mind on the Spirit is life and peace. For the mind that is set on the flesh is hostile to God, for it does not submit to God's law; indeed, it cannot. Those who are in the flesh cannot please God. You, however, are not in the flesh but in the Spirit, if in fact the Spirit of God dwells in you. Anyone who does not have the Spirit of Christ does not belong to him (Rom. 8:5-9)...

...he meant something far more fundamental and deep-seated than spiritual gift. Clearly, he did not mean that someone who has never 'spoken in tongues', exercised 'the gift of healing', and so on, is not a true believer. Of course not. But unless one has been regenerated by the Spirit, convicted of sin and brought to saving repentance and trust in Christ, and is, by walking in the Spirit, keeping in step with the Spirit (Gal. 5:16,25), being transformed into conformity to Christ, he is, as yet, unconverted, he is powerless, spiritually speaking:

Truly, truly, I say to you, unless one is born again he cannot see the kingdom of God... Truly, truly, I say to you, unless one is born of water[2] and the Spirit, he cannot enter the kingdom of God. That which is born of the flesh is flesh, and that which is born of the Spirit is spirit. Do not marvel that I said to you: 'You must be born again'. The wind blows where it wishes, and you hear its sound, but you do not know where it comes from or where it goes. So it is with everyone who is born of the Spirit (John 3:3-8).

All that the Father gives me will come to me, and whoever comes to me I will never cast out... No one can come to me unless the Father who sent me draws him. And I will raise him up on the last day. It is written in the prophets: 'And they will all be taught by God'. Everyone who has heard and learned from the Father comes to me (John 6:37,44-45).

On the last day of the feast, the great day, Jesus stood up and cried out: 'If anyone thirsts, let him come to me and drink. Whoever believes in me, as the Scripture has said, 'Out of his heart will flow rivers of living water'. Now this he said about the Spirit, whom those who believed in him were to receive, for as yet the Spirit had not been given, because Jesus was not yet glorified (John 7:37-39).

I will ask the Father, and he will give you another Helper, to be with you forever, even the Spirit of truth, whom the world cannot receive, because it neither sees him nor knows him. You know him, for he dwells with you and will be in you (John 14:16-17).

When he comes, he will convict the world concerning sin... because they do not believe in me (John 16:8-9).

My brothers, you... have died to the law through the body of Christ, so that you may belong to another, to him who has been raised from the dead, in order that we may bear fruit for God. For while we were living in the flesh, our sinful passions, aroused by the law, were at work in our members to bear fruit for death. But now we are released from the law, having died to that which held us captive, so

---

[2] This is not a reference to baptism, any more than 'fire' is a reference to roasting (Matt. 3:11). See my *Infant*.

that we serve in the new way of the Spirit and not in the old way of the written code (Rom. 7:4-6).

There is therefore now no condemnation for those who are in Christ Jesus. For the law of the Spirit of life has set you free in Christ Jesus from the law of sin and death. For God has done what the law, weakened by the flesh, could not do. By sending his own Son in the likeness of sinful flesh and for sin, he condemned sin in the flesh, in order that the righteous requirement of the law might be fulfilled in us, who walk not according to the flesh but according to the Spirit. For those who live according to the flesh set their minds on the things of the flesh, but those who live according to the Spirit set their minds on the things of the Spirit. For to set the mind on the flesh is death, but to set the mind on the Spirit is life and peace. For the mind that is set on the flesh is hostile to God, for it does not submit to God's law; indeed, it cannot. Those who are in the flesh cannot please God.
You, however, are not in the flesh but in the Spirit, if in fact the Spirit of God dwells in you. Anyone who does not have the Spirit of Christ does not belong to him. But if Christ is in you, although the body is dead because of sin, the Spirit is life because of righteousness. If the Spirit of him who raised Jesus from the dead dwells in you, he who raised Christ Jesus from the dead will also give life to your mortal bodies through his Spirit who dwells in you (Rom. 8:1-11).

Those whom [God] foreknew he also predestined to be conformed to the image of his Son, in order that he might be the firstborn among many brothers. And those whom he predestined he also called, and those whom he called he also justified, and those whom he justified he also glorified (Rom. 8:29-30).

The natural person does not accept the things of the Spirit of God, for they are folly [foolishness] to him, and he is not able to understand them because they are spiritually discerned. The spiritual person... (1 Cor. 2:14-15).

Are we beginning to commend ourselves again? Or do we need, as some do, letters of recommendation to you, or from you? You yourselves are our letter of recommendation, written on our [or your] hearts, to be known and read by all. And you show that you are a letter

from Christ delivered by us, written not with ink but with the Spirit of the living God, not on tablets of stone but on tablets of human hearts.
Such is the confidence that we have through Christ toward God. Not that we are sufficient in ourselves to claim anything as coming from us, but our sufficiency is from God, who has made us sufficient to be ministers of a new covenant, not of the letter but of the Spirit. For the letter kills, but the Spirit gives life...
The Lord is the Spirit, and where the Spirit of the Lord is, there is freedom. And we all, with unveiled face, beholding the glory of the Lord, are being transformed into the same image from one degree of glory to another. For this comes from the Lord who is the Spirit (2 Cor. 3:1-18).

Walk by the Spirit, and you will not gratify the desires of the flesh. For the desires of the flesh are against the Spirit, and the desires of the Spirit are against the flesh, for these are opposed to each other, to keep you from doing the things you want to do. But if you are led by the Spirit, you are not under the law. Now the works of the flesh are evident... I warn you, as I warned you before, that those who do such things will not inherit the kingdom of God. But the fruit of the Spirit is... against such things there is no law. And those who belong to Christ Jesus have crucified the flesh with its passions and desires. If we live by the Spirit, let us also keep in step with the Spirit. Let us not become conceited, provoking one another, envying one another (Gal. 5:16-26).

That I may know him and the power of his resurrection, and may share his sufferings, becoming like him in his death (Phil. 3:10).

Is there any question, then, that when Paul was addressing the Corinthians as to whether or not the super-apostles had power (1 Cor. 4:20), he was not calling into question merely their preaching ability? He allowed that they might have 'the gift of the gab' or eloquence (1 Cor. 2:1-5), but did they have 'power'? Did their preaching lead to real conversions? On a more penetrating level, were they regenerate? Were they themselves living in the power of the Spirit? Did they even have the Spirit? Were they in the kingdom? Or was it all a show, outward, a matter of talk and appearance? Deeply serious questions! That was the issue; that was Paul's challenge:

> Some are arrogant, as though I were not coming to you. But I will come to you soon, if the Lord wills, and I will find out not the talk of these arrogant people but their power. For the kingdom of God does not consist in talk but in power (1 Cor. 4:18-20).

So what is this 'power' that makes a profession of Christ real? The key passage must be Romans 2:28-29. Here it is again:

> No one is a Jew who is merely one outwardly, nor is circumcision outward and physical. But a Jew is one inwardly, and circumcision is a matter of the heart, by the Spirit, not by the letter. His praise is not from man but from God (Rom. 2:28-29).

The heart – what God sees, not what man sees – that is key. As God told Samuel when he was looking for a prospective king:

> Do not look on his appearance or on the height of his [that is, Eliab's] stature, because I have rejected him. For the LORD sees not as man sees: man looks on the outward appearance, but the LORD looks on the heart (1 Sam. 16:7).

The sinner needs a new heart. Enter the Holy Spirit. As Jesus said, he – and he alone – has the power to take dead sinners and make them into living saints. In exercising his sovereign power, he removes the heart of stone from the sinner, removes the deadness, and implants a living heart, a living mind, a new mind, a new disposition, a new attitude, a new spirit. He makes the spiritually dead sinner to come to life, and then live in obedience to Christ in his law.[3] As God declared through the prophet:

---

[3] To make this section complete, I re-quote some earlier passages when required.

I will give them one heart, and a new spirit I will put within them. I will remove the heart of stone from their flesh and give them a heart of flesh, that they may walk in my statutes and keep my rules and obey them. And they shall be my people, and I will be their God (Ezek. 11:19-20).

And he – both God and the prophet – repeated the point:

I will give you a new heart, and a new spirit I will put within you. And I will remove the heart of stone from your flesh and give you a heart of flesh. And I will put my Spirit within you, and cause you to walk in my statutes and be careful to obey my just decrees (Ezek. 36:26-27).[4]

As Christ told Nicodemus:

Truly, truly, I say to you, unless one is born again he cannot see the kingdom of God.

Nicodemus said to him:

How can a man be born when he is old? Can he enter a second time into his mother's womb and be born?

Jesus answered:

Truly, truly, I say to you, unless one is born of water[5] and the Spirit, he cannot enter the kingdom of God. That which is born of the flesh is flesh, and that which is born of the Spirit is spirit. Do not marvel that I said to you: 'You must be born again'. The wind blows where it wishes, and you hear its sound, but you do not know where it comes from or where it goes. So it is with everyone who is born of the Spirit (John 3:3-8).

So, combining John 3:3-8 and Ezekiel 11:19-20; 36:26-27 (among other passages), it is clear that nothing but sovereign regeneration by the Spirit will do. That is the 'power' in question. Unless we're born again, we will never see the kingdom. It's only born-again sinners who feel and know

---

[4] In new-covenant terms, these 'just decrees' are gospel commands.
[5] This 'water' does not refer to baptism. As 'fire' (Matt. 3:11), it speaks of the purifying, cleansing power and effect of regeneration. See my *Infant*.

that they are sinners. That's one mark of regeneration – conviction of sin (John 16:8-9). But it does not stop there. It is only regenerate sinners who actually repent of their sins before God. Again, only regenerate sinners can, by God's grace, by the work of the Spirit, believe on the Lord Jesus Christ, trust him, and receive him as their Saviour and Lord, and so love and obey him. Moreover, not only can they trust Christ; by God's Spirit that is what they do. They are made a new creation (Matt. 19:25-26; John 1:10-13; 6:63-65; 2 Cor. 5:17; Eph. 2:1-10; Col. 2:13; Tit. 3:4-7; 1 Pet. 1:2-3,23-25; 1 John 3:9-10; 4:7-8; 5:1-5, for instance), and live by the Spirit (Gal. 5:16,25) with Christ as King, Lord and God (John 20:28-29; Acts 17:7; 1 Tim. 1:17; 6:15; Heb. 1:8; Rev. 19:16), being made increasingly to conform to Christ (Rom. 8:29-30).

To accomplish all that requires infinite power – and nothing but the invincible power of the Spirit will do; nothing else, nothing less than the Spirit's power can effect it. Nobody but the Spirit can change dead sinners into living saints. Legal preaching, legal prescription, inducing fear – so common by false teachers in apostolic days, and still widespread – cannot do it.[6] Churchianity will not do it; churchianity can't do it. Religion is useless, and worse – it is fatal. Sadly, today, many people (including many evangelicals) are becoming more and more accustomed to thinking that church attendance, that churchianity, that coached conformity and religiosity will somehow do the job. It won't! No! Not religion, but regeneration! Regeneration by the sovereign grace and power of the Holy Spirit – the only one who can take dead sinners and turn them into living saints – is essential: 'You must be born again'. Mere appearance is useless.

> The LORD your God will circumcise your heart and the heart of your offspring, so that you will love the LORD

---

[6] See my *False*.

your God with all your heart and with all your soul, that
you may live (Deut. 30:6).

Whatever that meant for Israel in the old covenant...

> No one can say 'Jesus is Lord' except in the Holy Spirit (1
> Cor. 12:3).

Well, he can – but not truly, sincerely, really. After all, we
know that the natural man thinks that spiritual things are
foolish; he even hates them:

> The natural person does not accept the things of the Spirit
> of God, for they are folly [foolishness] to him, and he is not
> able to understand them because they are spiritually
> discerned. The spiritual person... (1 Cor. 2:14-15).[7]

> The mind that is set on the flesh [that is, the carnal mind,
> the mind of a natural man] is hostile to God, for it does not
> submit to God's law; indeed, it cannot (Rom. 8:7).

Consequently, 'power' is the key issue – not talk, not
outward show, form, not conformity, but power. And that
power is supplied only by the Spirit – not by man, his wit,
his ingenuity, his skill at 're-engineering' the *ekklēsia*,[8] his
programs or whatever – but, I say again, by the Spirit, and
only by the Spirit. Even in the old covenant, the Jews were
told this:

> Not by might, nor by [human] power, but by my Spirit, says
> the LORD of hosts (Zech. 4:6).

> I will have mercy on the house of Judah, and I will save
> them by the LORD their God. I will not save them by bow
> or by sword or by war or by horses or by horsemen (Hos.
> 1:7).

> 'Ah, stubborn children', declares the LORD, 'who carry out
> a plan, but not mine, and who make an alliance [weave a
> web], but not of my Spirit, that they may add sin to sin;
> who set out to go down to Egypt, without asking for my

---

[7] See my 'Natural & Spiritual' on my sermonaudio.com and
YouTube pages.
[8] See my *Relationship*.

direction, to take refuge in the protection of Pharaoh and to seek shelter in the shadow of Egypt! Therefore shall the protection of Pharaoh turn to your shame, and the shelter in the shadow of Egypt to your humiliation. For though his officials are at Zoan and his envoys reach Hanes, everyone comes to shame through a people that cannot profit them, that brings neither help nor profit, but shame and disgrace' (Isa. 30:1-5).[9]

How much more so today!

---

[9] See my *Evangelicals*.

Poison at the Root

We need, first of all, to get to the root.

Getting to the root

What, in Scripture, is the great antithesis to 'Spirit'? It is 'flesh'. Sometimes this dependence on 'flesh' is spoken of in terms of 'law' or 'works'.[1] Of course, in the early days of the new covenant this dependence was often shown by a reversion to Judaism, but the principle applies much wider than that. Moreover, the repudiation of the Spirit need not always be overt.

We know that Scripture starkly contrasts the Spirit and the flesh, the Spirit and law. As we have seen:

> There is therefore now no condemnation for those who are in Christ Jesus. For the law of the Spirit of life has set you free in Christ Jesus from the law of sin and death. For God has done what the law, weakened by the flesh, could not do. By sending his own Son in the likeness of sinful flesh and for sin, he condemned sin in the flesh, in order that the righteous requirement of the law might be fulfilled in us, who walk not according to the flesh but according to the Spirit. For those who live according to the flesh set their minds on the things of the flesh, but those who live according to the Spirit set their minds on the things of the Spirit. For to set the mind on the flesh is death, but to set the mind on the Spirit is life and peace. For the mind that is set on the flesh is hostile to God, for it does not submit to God's law; indeed, it cannot. Those who are in the flesh cannot please God. You, however, are not in the flesh but in the Spirit, if in fact the Spirit of God dwells in you. Anyone who does not have the Spirit of Christ does not belong to him (Rom. 8:1-9).

We know that a person is not justified by works of the law but through faith in Jesus Christ, so we also have believed

---

[1] See my 'Paul's Answer: The Spirit' in my *False*.

in Christ Jesus, in order to be justified by faith in Christ and not by works of the law, because by works of the law no one will be justified...

O foolish Galatians! Who has bewitched you? It was before your eyes that Jesus Christ was publicly portrayed as crucified. Let me ask you only this: Did you receive the Spirit by works of the law or by hearing with faith? Are you so foolish? Having begun by the Spirit, are you now being perfected by the flesh?... Does he who supplies the Spirit to you and works miracles among you do so by works of the law, or by hearing with faith...? (Gal. 2:16; 3:1-5).

Just as at that time [that is, in the days of Ishmael and Isaac] he who was born according to the flesh persecuted him who was born according to the Spirit, so also it is now (Gal. 4:29).

You are severed from Christ, you who would be justified by the law; you have fallen away from grace. For through the Spirit, by faith, we ourselves eagerly wait for the hope of righteousness...

Walk by the Spirit, and you will not gratify the desires of the flesh. For the desires of the flesh are against the Spirit, and the desires of the Spirit are against the flesh, for these are opposed to each other, to keep you from doing the things you want to do. But if you are led by the Spirit, you are not under the law. Now the works of the flesh are evident... I warn you, as I warned you before, that those who do such things will not inherit the kingdom of God. But the fruit of the Spirit is... against such things there is no law. And those who belong to Christ Jesus have crucified the flesh with its passions and desires. If we live by the Spirit, let us also keep in step with the Spirit. Let us not become conceited, provoking one another, envying one another (Gal. 5:4-5,16-26).

The one who sows to his own flesh will from the flesh reap corruption, but the one who sows to the Spirit will from the Spirit reap eternal life... Those who want to make a good showing in the flesh... would force you to be circumcised, and only in order that they may not be persecuted for the cross of Christ. For even those who are circumcised do not themselves keep the law, but they desire to have you circumcised that they may boast in your flesh. But far be it from me to boast except in the cross of our Lord Jesus Christ, by which the world has been crucified to me, and I to the world. For neither circumcision counts for anything, nor uncircumcision, but a new creation (Gal. 6:8,12-15).

In light of such passages, look again at this:

No one is a Jew who is merely one outwardly, nor is circumcision outward and physical. But a Jew is one inwardly, and circumcision is a matter of the heart, by the Spirit, not by the letter. His praise is not from man but from God (Rom. 2:28-29).

By works of the law no human being will be justified in his sight... But now the righteousness of God has been manifested apart from the law, although the law and the prophets bear witness to it – the righteousness of God through faith in Jesus Christ for all who believe... One is justified by faith apart from works of the law (Rom. 3:20-22,28).

Put on the Lord Jesus Christ, and make no provision for the flesh (Rom.13:14).

Flesh and blood cannot inherit the kingdom of God (1 Cor. 15:50).

You show that you are a letter from Christ delivered by us, written not with ink but with the Spirit of the living God, not on tablets of stone but on tablets of human hearts. Such is the confidence that we have through Christ toward God. Not that we are sufficient in ourselves to claim anything as coming from us, but our sufficiency is from God, who has made us sufficient to be ministers of a new covenant, not of the letter but of the Spirit. For the letter kills, but the Spirit gives life (2 Cor. 3:3-6).

We all... beholding the glory of the Lord, are being transformed into the same image from one degree of glory to another. For this comes from the Lord who is the Spirit (2 Cor. 3:18).

We regard no one according to the flesh. Even though we once regarded Christ according to the flesh, we regard him thus no longer. Therefore, if anyone is in Christ, he is a new creation. The old has passed away; behold, the new has come. All this is from God, who through Christ reconciled us to himself (2 Cor. 5:16-18).

We are the circumcision, who worship by the Spirit of God and glory in Christ Jesus and put no confidence in the flesh (Phil. 3:3).

Consequently, to 'repudiate the power', to repudiate the Spirit, is to encourage the flesh, to promote the law – *and* **vice-versa**. Men are guilty of 'having the appearance of godliness, but denying its power' when they give the least encouragement to the notion that 'godliness' (in all its aspects) can be obtained in any other way than by the power of the Spirit.

We need to be clear. I spoke of 'godliness in all its aspects'. While it is true that we are speaking about justification, we must not confine Paul's warning to Timothy – and all the apostolic warnings about reversion to the law – to justification; sanctification – both positional and progressive[2] – is also in view.[3]

As I say, in the apostolic days, the issue concerning law showed itself in a widespread effort to return to Judaism – hence, for instance, the letter to the Hebrews.[4] Today, while we should not be thinking only in terms of a return to Judaism – although, strident calls for 'a return to Jewish roots' is far from unknown (indeed, I fear it is on the rise) – whenever eyes are taken away from Christ and centred on flesh, works or law, we are coming face to face with the 'repudiation of the Spirit'. And that is far from uncommon![5]

* * *

Now for the poison.

---

[2] See my *Fivefold*; *Positional*.
[3] See my *Christ*; *False*.
[4] But see also Romans; 2 Corinthians; Galatians; Ephesians; Philippians, Colossians; 1 Peter. See my *False*.
[5] See my *False*.

We have not exhausted Paul's warning to Timothy about those:

> ...having the appearance of godliness, but denying its power (2 Tim. 3:5).

One of the marks of this age is that there will those who profess Christ – they have 'the appearance of godliness' – but they lack the reality, they do not have its power.

But Paul did not actually say that; he probed much deeper – and in two respects.

First, the apostle was speaking of those who, while they have a show of spirituality, not only lack the Spirit, but they *deny* the power, they *deny* the Spirit. The word means 'deny, repudiate, oppose, abrogate, forsake, or renounce'. Not only do such people not have the power of the Spirit, but they actually hate all talk of it, they resist it, they repudiate it; they decidedly prefer the veneer, the varnish, to the reality, and they are prepared to fight for it.

Secondly, Paul tells Timothy: 'Avoid such people' (2 Tim. 3:5); that is, shun them, have nothing to do with them. Timothy must not tolerate and accommodate such, he must not cosy up to them, but shun them; indeed, keep on shunning them: 'be you shunning'.

In short, Paul says that this age will be marked by those who resist the Spirit. Moreover, he says, the duty, the obligation, laid on true believers, the *ekklēsia*, does not stop at guarding against such: believers must shun them. Certainly they must not accept, tolerate or accommodate them.

This, of course, is not the only scriptural warning about resisting the Spirit, and how to deal with it. Stephen was blunt:

> You stiff-necked people, uncircumcised in heart and ears, you always resist the Holy Spirit (Acts 7:51).

Stephen had observed the practice. But he did not stop there. He confronted it – at huge personal risk. Indeed, he paid the ultimate price.

Paul knew that believers always stand in risk of resisting the Spirit – that is why he commanded believers:

> Do not grieve the Holy Spirit of God (Eph. 4:30).

> Do not quench the Spirit (1 Thess. 5:19).

D.Martyn Lloyd-Jones pulled no punches over the issue. Here are two extracts from the MLJ Trust – introductory remarks outlining two sermons:

> In this sermon on Ephesians 6:10-13 titled 'Quenching the Spirit (1)', Dr Martyn Lloyd-Jones makes the bold claim that the church's quenching of the Holy Spirit hinders it more than anything else. What is quenching the Spirit? In a desire to avoid making Christianity reliant on subjective religious experiences, many Christians leave no room for the work and the ministry of the Holy Spirit in their lives. This is quenching the Holy Spirit.

I break in to say that this is not the only way in which to quench the Spirit! It is not unknown for law-teachers, for instance, while they pay lip service to the Spirit, to make the Spirit little more than a doctrinal principle or theological chess-piece than a felt reality, than a vital part of the believer's daily experience.

The blurb continued:

> The Bible tells [us] that the Holy Spirit is a person who indwells all who believe. The church of today ought to look at the early church found in Acts to see what it looks like to rely on the Holy Spirit for power and guidance. What are the practical applications of this discourse[6] on Ephesians 6:10–13? Christians should seek to look to the Holy Spirit to empower their ministries and lives as they follow Jesus Christ. The church as a whole should look to the guidance

---

[6] Original 'message'. I prefer to keep this for the import of actual Scripture, not a man's discourse on a scripture.

of the Holy Spirit as he enables[7] Christians to understand the gospel and God's word. Christians must not overreact against those who abuse the Bible's teaching on the Holy Spirit by suppressing what the Bible does teach about the Holy Spirit and his ministry in the church.

And:

In his sermon on Ephesians 6:10-13 titled 'Quenching the Spirit (2)', Dr Martyn Lloyd-Jones offers a challenging and convicting discourse[8] to the church today: beware of quenching the Spirit. Quenching the Holy Spirit is one of the ways the devil works in believers' lives in order to make their Christian life ineffectual and lacking power. Dr Lloyd-Jones diagnoses the problem by looking at the Scriptures and noting that the person filled with the Spirit knows their doctrine, has a love and warmth about them, and has the power of the Holy Spirit. Dr Lloyd-Jones then proceeds to offer application for how one can be guilty of quenching the Spirit. He attacks such practices as formalism in the church...[9] as well as a general resistance of the Spirit's prompting.[10]

Quenching the Spirit is the poison at the root.

---

[7] Original 'allows'. Far too weak.
[8] See previous note but one.
[9] I have omitted 'conflating regeneration and the baptism of the Spirit'. I disagree with Lloyd-Jones' view of spiritual baptism.
[10] MLJ Trust website.

Application

When Paul told Timothy:

> Understand this, that in the last days [that is, during this gospel age][1] there will come times of difficulty. For people will be lovers of self, lovers of money, proud, arrogant, abusive, disobedient to their parents, ungrateful, unholy, heartless, unappeasable, slanderous, without self-control, brutal, not loving good, treacherous, reckless, swollen with conceit, lovers of pleasure rather than lovers of God, having the appearance of godliness, but denying its power. Avoid such people (2 Tim. 3:1-5)...

...he was not telling him – as a stimulus to carnal speculation – that dreadful apostasy would mark the final, closing years of this age; that is, its last three and a half, or seven, years (depending on which prophetic scheme you hold). For a start, how could Timothy avoid such people if they would only exist 2000 or more years after he had died? In any case, Romans 1:18-32, where Paul said much the same thing to the Romans, is in the present or past tense. No, whatever it was that Paul was warning Timothy about was already present – and prevalent – in first-century Ephesus. And not only there and at that time. The apostle was spelling out what all believers must expect throughout this age.[2]

How frequently the apostles sounded this warning about apostasy, *apostasy even in their days!* Consider, for instance, Acts 20:17-31; Galatians 1:6; 1 Timothy 1:19-20; 2 Timothy 4:1-4; Hebrews; 2 Peter 2:1-22; 1 John 2:19; Jude; Revelation 2 & 3. Take the *ekklēsia* at Ephesus (the warning in Acts 20, the letter and, finally, Revelation 2:1-7); how quickly it declined!

---

[1] See, for instance, Acts 2:17; 1 Cor. 10:11; Heb. 1:2; 1 Pet. 1:20; 1 John 2:18.

[2] See the previous note.

Then again, when Paul told the Corinthians that 'the kingdom of God does not consist in talk but in power', he was laying down a general principle, a principle which is always true, which always applies. It applied in Paul's day; it applies today. Indeed, Paul was doing the same as Christ in John 3:3-8. Nicodemus wanted a pleasant conversation about spiritual matters. Christ would have none of it! 'You must be born again!' he thundered. 'Until you are born again, unless you are born again, you will never see – never even see, let alone enter – the kingdom!'. Flesh remains flesh until the man is regenerated and made spiritual. And as Paul told the Corinthians: 'Until you are regenerate, spiritual matters will be foolishness to you'. His actual words read:

> The natural person [the unregenerate man] does not accept the things of the Spirit of God, for they are folly [foolishness] to him, and he is not able to understand them because they are spiritually discerned (1 Cor. 2:14).

That's not the least of it:

> The carnal mind [the mind, the thinking, the understanding, of the natural man, the unregenerate] is enmity against God (Rom. 8:7).

And all that applies today. Since the fall of Adam, there has never been a single human being born of a father and mother to whom it has not applied. It always applies. Flesh is always flesh, and natural man, an unregenerate man, is always in Adam until he is regenerated by the sovereign Spirit of God and transformed (Col. 1:13), made spiritual, united to Christ by faith:

> Just as sin came into the world through one man, and death through sin, and so death spread to all men because all sinned – for sin indeed was in the world before the law was given, but sin is not counted where there is no law. Yet death reigned from Adam to Moses, even over those whose sinning was not like the transgression of Adam, who was a type of the one who was to come.
> But the free gift is not like the trespass. For if many died through one man's trespass, much more have the grace of

God and the free gift by the grace of that one man Jesus
Christ abounded for many. And the free gift is not like the
result of that one man's sin. For the judgment following one
trespass brought condemnation, but the free gift following
many trespasses brought justification. For if, because of one
man's trespass, death reigned through that one man, much
more will those who receive the abundance of grace and the
free gift of righteousness reign in life through the one man
Jesus Christ.
Therefore, as one trespass led to condemnation for all men,
so one act of righteousness leads to justification and life for
all men. For as by the one man's disobedience the many
were made sinners, so by the one man's obedience the
many will be made righteous. Now the law came in to
increase the trespass, but where sin increased, grace
abounded all the more, so that, as sin reigned in death,
grace also might reign through righteousness leading to
eternal life through Jesus Christ our Lord (Rom. 5:12-21).

For as in Adam all die, so also in Christ shall all be made
alive.... Thus it is written: 'The first man Adam became a
living being'; the last Adam [that is, Christ] became a life-
giving spirit. But it is not the spiritual that is first but the
natural, and then the spiritual. The first man was from the
earth, a man of dust; the second man is from heaven. As
was the man of dust, so also are those who are of the dust,
and as is the man of heaven, so also are those who are of
heaven. Just as we have borne the image of the man of dust,
we shall also bear the image of the man of heaven. I tell
you this, brothers: flesh and blood cannot inherit the
kingdom of God, nor does the perishable inherit the
imperishable (1 Cor. 15:22,45-50).

Putting all this together, we know that throughout this age,
churches have been, will be – *and are being at this very
moment* – plagued by those who mistake veneer – image and
chat, appearance, show – for reality – true spirituality,
spiritual power. Indeed, the grim underlying principle is ever
with us: such people 'repudiate true spiritual power'.
Moreover, the apostle's command to true believers still
stands: 'avoid such people'. This solemn teaching, with its
associated command, therefore, is always relevant – never
more so than today. I am convinced that we, as

contemporary evangelicals, desperately need to face it, and, having faced it for ourselves, we must go on to make sure that we confront professing believers attending our churches – as well as rank unbelievers – with it. Nothing – nothing – is more necessary today.

Why? Why, especially, today?

As I have explained elsewhere,[3] I am convinced that most contemporary believers are becoming increasingly enmeshed in a system which has utterly transformed the new-covenant status and function of the *ekklēsia*. Utterly transformed it. If Paul came on the scene today, he simply would not recognise today's goings-on. We can so easily fool ourselves. We need to grasp the damage Christendom has inflicted; it is has turned many churches into little more than local outlets for a global corporation, a plush shopping mall, an amusement arcade or a would-be glitzy theatre of entertainment – tinged with 'spirituality', of course.

The upshot, in brief, is that instead of the *ekklēsia* being – as it ought to be – a living, active, vital society of believers, separate from the world, the modern Christendom-church is doing all it can to break down the God-ordained gulf between the *ekklēsia* and the world in order to attract as many unbelievers as it can into prolonged church-attendance in order to evangelise them. The ultimate motive may be good – if true conversion *is* the motive, then the motive *is* good – but the scheme is utterly unbiblical.[4] I am convinced that evangelical Christendom, by such methods, is actually encouraging the wholesale confusion of veneer for reality, varnish for substance, and in so doing is – to put it no stronger – actually guilty of encouraging the repudiation of the Spirit, the proliferation of natural men and women who think, and who are treated as, spiritual.

---

[3] *Attracting*; *Relationship*; *Evangelicals Warned*.
[4] For my arguments, please see my works listed in the previous note.

As a consequence, an increasing number of unbelievers are being absorbed into Christendom-church attendance – and, in many cases, church-participation – yet remain unconverted, still dead in sin. Worse still, they can remain in that condition without ever being really, powerfully, directly, bluntly, passionately confronted with the principle that 'the kingdom of God does not consist in talk but in power'; or, to apply the dictum to today's circumstances, they are rarely, if ever, confronted with the fact that 'the kingdom of God does not consist in church attendance, and participation in church activity, in being able to parrot a catechism or credal statement learnt by rote, but in power, in reality, in a felt-experience of Christ'. Confrontation is out! Confrontation would work directly against the overriding principle of attracting attenders. Why drive them away? Why raise any barrier?[5] The grievous truth is, many contemporary evangelicals are directly encouraging – promoting – *within their churches*, this classic sign of apostasy in this age, 'the last days', about which Paul warned Timothy: 'having the appearance of godliness, but denying its power'.

Notice they 'having the appearance of godliness, but denying its power' is the climax of Paul's catalogue of the marks of declension (2 Tim. 3:1-5)! That's the climax: a form or show of spirituality, without the actual experience of it, actually while repudiating it. And I say, that is the very thing that is being actively and energetically encouraged by many contemporary evangelical churches. Think of it! And that is why I say that we evangelicals need to face the blunt apostolic truth that 'the kingdom of God does not consist in talk but in power'. And, having faced it, we need to retrace our steps, put our house in order, and act in accordance with new-covenant principles. Moreover, as I have said, we need to confront professors and unbelievers with the principle.

Nothing, in my opinion, is more urgent.

---

[5] See my *To Confront?*

This is so important, I want to expose it even further. As I have said, we live in a time when many believers are preoccupied with packing consumers into church attendance, holding them, taking them through a training course, coaching them into giving the right answers so that they can pass muster in any investigation as prospective church members. This last is nothing new – the descendants of the New England settlers (who intended to set up a puritan colony) became masters of the art, virtually cramming or coaching candidates, making them as near word-perfect as possible, for an examination pass.[6] The cry today is: 'Come to church' rather than 'Come to Christ'.[7] Moreover, a great deal of the current gospel-preaching is straight Sandemanianism.[8] But conformity to rules, and mere head-knowledge of facts, will never produce spirituality:

> ...regulations... 'Do not handle, Do not taste, Do not touch' (referring to things that all perish as they are used) – according to human precepts and teachings... have indeed an appearance of wisdom in promoting self-made religion and asceticism and severity to the body, but they are of no value in stopping the indulgence of the flesh (Col. 2:20-23).

We must call a spade a spade. Charles Ellicott on 2 Timothy 3:5:

> These, by claiming the title of Christians, wearing before men the uniform of Christ, but by their lives dishonouring his name, did the gravest injury to the holy Christian cause.

---

[6] When my son was taking his 'O' level examination in Geography, I knew that because of the inadequacy of the preparation provided by his teacher, he was certain to fail. I asked another teacher for advice; although, of course, he had not seen the paper, as an experienced teacher he was able to give me six topics he advised I should cover. The evening before the examination, I crammed those six topics into my son's head. The next day he passed his examination; I could have passed it. The day after, I would have failed. For the spiritual equivalent – coaching people to give the right answers – see my *Four*; *Assurance*; *The Secret*; *Christ*; *Infant*.
[7] See my *In Church?*
[8] See my *The Secret*.

Another dreary catalogue of vices... Paul gives in the [letter] to the Romans (Rom. 1:29*ff.*); but in that passage he paints the sins of paganism. Here he describes the characteristics of a new paganism, which went under the name of Christianity.

That's it in a nutshell: 'a new paganism, which went under the name of Christianity'. Think of that!

All this provokes some very serious questions, questions I must put to myself – and, of course, questions you, reader, must put to yourself.

Is my spirituality just a matter of talk, of chat? That is, do I know – in my head – the leading points of the gospel? Do I like to talk about them; even, do I *love* to talk about them, but am I an utter stranger to the felt experience – the inward power – of them?

J.C.Ryle wrote:

> What do I mean when I speak of formal spirituality?[9] This is a point that must be made clear. Thousands, I suspect, know nothing about it. Without a distinct understanding of this point, my whole paper will be useless. My first step shall be to paint, describe and define. When a man is a Christian in name only – and not in reality; in outward things only – and not in his inward feelings; in profession only – and not in practice; when his Christianity, in short, is a mere matter of form, or fashion, or custom without any influence on his heart or life – in such a case as this, the man has what I call a 'formal spiritual profession'. He possesses indeed the form, or husk, or skin of spiritual profession – but he does not possess its substance or its power.
>
> Look, for example, at those thousands of people whose whole spiritual profession seems to consist in keeping religious ceremonies and ordinances. They attend regularly on public worship.[10] They go regularly to the Lord's table. But they never get any further. They know nothing of

---

[9] Original 'religion'. This note applies throughout this booklet.
[10] That is, church attendance. See my *Public*.

experimental Christianity. They are not familiar with the Scriptures – and take no delight in reading them. They do not separate themselves from the ways of the world. They draw no distinction between godliness and ungodliness in their friendships, or matrimonial alliances. They care little or nothing about the distinctive doctrines of the gospel. They appear utterly indifferent as to what they hear preached. You may be in their company for weeks, and for anything you may hear or see – you might suppose they were infidels! What can be said about these people? They are Christians undoubted, by profession; and yet there is neither heart nor life in their Christianity. There is but one thing to be said about them: They are formal Christians – their spiritual profession is a mere form!

Look in another direction, at those hundreds of people whose whole spiritual profession seems to consist in talk and high profession. They know the theory of the gospel with their heads, and profess to delight in evangelical doctrine. They can say much about the 'soundness' of their own views, and the 'darkness' of all who disagree with them; but they never get any further! When you examine their inner lives – you find that they know nothing of practical godliness... They are formal Christians – their spiritual profession is an empty form!

The question deserves especial notice in this age of the church and world. Never since the Lord Jesus Christ left the earth, was there so much formality and false profession, as there is at the present day. Now, if ever, we ought to examine ourselves, and search our spiritual profession, that we may know of what sort it is. Reader, let us find out whether our Christianity is a thing of form – or a thing of heart.[11]

As Joseph Hart said, and said more briefly than Ryle, true belief is more than notion:

> *Let us ask th'important question,*
> *(Brethren, be not too secure),*
> *What it is to be a Christian?*
> *How we may our hearts assure!*
> *Vain is all our best devotion,*
> *If on false foundations built:*

---

[11] J.C.Ryle: 'Formal Religion', 1878.

> *True professed Christianity's*[12] *more than notion;*
> *Something must be known and felt.*

Just so! Something must be *known* **and** *felt*. Better: *Someone* must be known, and our relationship to him must be felt!

In one of its many editions, in a footnote at the end of John Bunyan's *The Pilgrim's Progress,*[13] the editor added some words from William Mason:

> Does Christ dwell in my heart by faith? Am I a new creature in him? Do I look alone to Christ for righteousness, and depend only on him for holiness? Is he the only hope of my soul, and the only confidence of my heart? And do I desire to be found in him; knowing by the word, and feeling by the teaching of his Spirit, that I am totally lost in myself? Thus, is Christ formed in me, the only hope of glory? Do I study to please him, as well as hope to enjoy him? Is fellowship with God the Father, and his Son, Jesus Christ, so prized by me, as to seek it, and to esteem it above all things? If so, though I may find all things in nature, in the world, and from Satan, continually opposing this, yet I am in Christ the way, and he is in me the truth and the life.

The editor himself added:

> How far may such an one go? [He called this:] This important question... They may become preachers and ministers of the gospel, with rare gifts, and a fluent tongue, like an angel, to speak of the hidden mysteries; but may die under the curse. They may have the gifts of the Spirit and prophecy, and be but a Balaam. They may stand thus until Christ comes and reveals them. They may, with confidence, say, Lord, Lord, have we not eaten and drank in your presence, and taught in your name, and in your name have cast out devils? and yet, poor creatures, be shut out!

Let me close this chapter – indeed, the main part of my book – with this solemn, but vital, call from William Gadsby:

---

[12] Original 'religion'.

[13] For more from *The Pilgrim's Progress*, see Appendix 1.

Application

Pause my soul! and ask the question,
Are you ready to meet God?
Am I made a real Christian,
Washed in the Redeemer's blood?
Have I union
With the church's living Head?

Am I quickened by his Spirit;
Live a life of faith and prayer?
Trusting wholly to his merit;
Casting on him all my care?
Daily longing
In his likeness to appear?

If my hope on Christ is stayèd,
Let him come when he thinks best;
O my soul be not dismayèd,
Lean upon his loving breast;
He will cheer you
With the smilings of his face.

But, if, still a total stranger
To his precious name and blood,
You are on the brink of danger;
Can you face a holy God?
Think and tremble,
Death is now upon the road.

APPENDICES

Appendix 1: Bunyan on Power

The conversation between Faithful and Talkative, spiced with some remarks from Christian – which John Bunyan recorded in his *The Pilgrim's Progress* – must be a leading candidate for the most challenging, the most searching, part of the entire allegory. It is for me, at least.[1] The truth is, Bunyan was in reality giving us an exposition of – and, above all, an application of – Paul's declaration to the Corinthians:

> The kingdom of God does not consist in talk but in power (1 Cor. 4:20).

As I have explained, I am convinced that in these few words we have one of the most important of all the many gospel principles recorded in Scripture, principles such as:

> Truly, truly, I say to you, unless one is born again he cannot see the kingdom of God... Truly, truly, I say to you, unless one is born of water[2] and the Spirit, he cannot enter the kingdom of God. That which is born of the flesh is flesh, and that which is born of the Spirit is spirit. Do not marvel that I said to you: 'You must be born again'. The wind blows where it wishes, and you hear its sound, but you do not know where it comes from or where it goes. So it is with everyone who is born of the Spirit (John 3:3-8).

> Not everyone who says to me: 'Lord, Lord', will enter the kingdom of heaven, but the one who does the will of my Father who is in heaven. On that day many will say to me: 'Lord, Lord, did we not prophesy in your name, and cast out demons in your name, and do many mighty works in your name?' And then will I declare to them: 'I never knew

---

[1] The fact that librarians can stock *The Pilgrim's Progress* in the children's section, shows how little understanding of the gospel such people, in general, have.

[2] This is not a reference to baptism, any more than 'fire' is a reference to roasting (Matt. 3:11). See my *Infant*.

you; depart from me, you workers of lawlessness' (Matt. 7:21-23).

No one is a Jew who is merely one outwardly, nor is circumcision outward and physical. But a Jew is one inwardly, and circumcision is a matter of the heart, by the Spirit, not by the letter. His praise is not from man but from God (Rom. 2:28-29).

Anyone who does not have the Spirit of Christ does not belong to him (Rom. 8:9).

And that's just four of them.

In the conversation between Faithful and Talkative in his *The Pilgrim's Progress*, Bunyan set out the core principle of these passages.

Let me remind you it:

Moreover, I saw in my dream, [wrote Bunyan] that as they [that is, Christian (as he was by this stage) and Faithful] went on, Faithful, as he chanced to look on one side, saw a man whose name is Talkative walking at a distance besides them; for in this place, there was room enough for them all to walk. He was a tall man, and something more comely at a distance than at hand. To this man Faithful addressed himself in this manner:

FAITH. Friend... are you going to the heavenly country?
TALK. I am going to the same place.
FAITH. That is well; then I hope we may have your good company.
TALK. With a very good will, will I be your companion.
FAITH. Come on, then, and let us go together, and let us spend our time in discoursing of things that are profitable.
TALK. To talk of things that are good, to me is very acceptable, with you, or with any other; and I am glad that I have met with those that incline to so good a work; for, to speak the truth, there are but few that care thus to spend their time (as they are in their travels), but choose much rather to be speaking of things to no profit; and this has been a trouble to me.

FAITH. That is indeed a thing to be lamented; for what things so worthy of the use of the tongue and mouth of men on earth, as are the things of the God of heaven?

Bunyan was here drawing attention to a very common lack among professing believers; namely, an unwillingness or inability to engage in spiritual conversation. Yet this is one of the main ways in which believers grow in spirituality![3]

Bunyan went on, driving home the point:

TALK. I like you wonderful well, for your sayings are full of conviction; and I will add, what thing is so pleasant, and what so profitable, as to talk of the things of God? What things so pleasant (that is, if a man has any delight in things that are wonderful)? For instance, if a man does delight to talk of the history or the mystery of things; or if a man does love to talk of miracles, wonders, or signs, where shall he find things recorded so delightful, and so sweetly penned, as in the Holy Scripture?

FAITH. That is true; but to be profited by such things in our talk should be that which we design.

TALK. That is it that I said; for to talk of such things is most profitable; for by so doing, a man may get knowledge of many things; as of the vanity of earthly things, and the benefit of things above. Thus, in general, but more particularly, by this, a man may learn the necessity of the new birth; the insufficiency of our works; the need of Christ's righteousness, *etc*. Besides, by this a man may learn, by talk, what it is to repent, to believe, to pray, to suffer, or the like; by this also a man may learn what are the great promises and consolations of the gospel, to his own comfort. Further, by this a man may learn to refute false opinions, to vindicate the truth, and also to instruct the ignorant.

FAITH. All this is true, and glad am I to hear these things from you.

TALK. Alas! the want of this is the cause why so few understand the need of faith, and the necessity of a work of grace in their soul, in order to eternal life; but ignorantly

---

[3] See my *Priesthood*; *Sowed*.

live in the works of the law, by which a man can by no means obtain the kingdom of heaven.

FAITH. But, by your leave, heavenly knowledge of these is the gift of God; no man attains to them by human industry, or only by the talk of them.

TALK. All this I know very well. For a man can receive nothing, except it be given him from heaven; all is of grace, not of works. I could give you a hundred scriptures for the confirmation of this.

FAITH. Well, then, said Faithful, what is that one thing that we shall at this time found [base] our discourse upon?

TALK. What you will. I will talk of things heavenly, or things earthly; things moral, or things evangelical; things sacred, or things profane; things past, or things to come; things foreign, or things at home; things more essential, or things circumstantial; provided that all be done to our profit.

Faithful was greatly impressed with his companion:

Now did Faithful begin to wonder; and stepping to Christian (for he walked all this while by himself), he said to him (but softly): 'What a brave companion have we got! Surely this man will make a very excellent pilgrim'.

But Christian was not taken in:

CHR. At this Christian modestly smiled, and said: 'This man, with whom you are so taken, will beguile, with that tongue of his, twenty of them that know him not'.

FAITH. Do you know him, then?

CHR. Know him! Yes, better than he knows himself.

FAITH. Pray, what is he?

CHR. His name is Talkative; he dwells in our town; I wonder that you should be a stranger to him, only I consider that our town is large.

FAITH. Whose son is he? And whereabouts does he dwell?

CHR. He is the son of one Say-well; he dwelt in Prating Row; and he is known of all that are acquainted with him, by the name of Talkative in Prating Row; and notwithstanding his fine tongue, he is but a sorry fellow.

FAITH. Well, he seems to be a very pretty [fine] man.

CHR. That is, to them who have not thorough acquaintance with him; for he is best abroad; near home, he is ugly enough. Your saying that he is a pretty man, brings to my mind what I have observed in the work of the painter whose pictures show best at a distance, but, very near, more unpleasing.

Christian took Faithful aside, gave him some home truths by telling him plainly the kind of man he was dealing with; namely, that while Talkative said one thing, he did another; that while he knew how to talk about spiritual things, and could do so with eloquence, in truth he knew nothing of them by felt, inward experience. It was all chat; or, more precisely, mere chatter. Talkative was a fully paid-up member of the chattering class. He would have been a star performer on any TV chat show today, especially one of a religious flavour: a professional chatterer.

> FAITH. Say you so! then am I in this man greatly deceived.
> CHR. Deceived! you may be sure of it; remember the proverb: 'They say, and do not' (Matt. 23:3). But 'the kingdom of God is not in word, but in power' (1 Cor. 4:20). He talks of prayer, of repentance, of faith, and of the new birth; but he knows but only to talk of them.

This is the key moment, the crunch or biting point, in the episode; or, as my American friends would say, this is where the rubber hits the road: 'The kingdom of God does not consist in talk but in power' (1 Cor. 4:20).

Faithful, being convinced, wanted to know how he could best stop Talkative's chatter, and be rid of him:

> CHR. Take my advice, and do as I bid you, and you shall find that he will soon be sick of your company too, except God shall touch his heart, and turn it.
> FAITH. What would you have me to do?
> CHR. Why, go to him, and enter into some serious discourse about the power of professed Christianity;[4] and ask him plainly (when he has approved of it, for that he will) whether this thing be set up in his heart, house, or conversation [that is, his way of life, not merely his talk]?

---

[4] Original 'religion'. This note, or its equivalent, applies throughout my book.

Faithful took his friend's advice:

> FAITH. Then Faithful stepped forward again, and said to
> Talkative, Come, what cheer? How is it now?
> TALK. Thank you, well. I thought we should have had a
> great deal of talk by this time.
> FAITH. Well, if you will, we will fall to it now; and since
> you left it with me to state the question, let it be this: How
> does the saving grace of God reveal itself, when it is in the
> heart of man?
> TALK. I perceive then, that our talk must be about the
> power of things. Well, it is a very good question, and I shall
> be willing to answer you. And take my answer in brief,
> thus: *First*, Where the grace of work of God is in the heart,
> it causes there a great outcry against sin. *Secondly...*
> FAITH. No, hold, let us consider your first point before we
> go any further.[5] I think you should rather say: It shows itself
> by inclining the soul to abhor its sin.
> TALK. Why, what difference is there between crying out
> against, and abhorring of sin?
> FAITH. O! a great deal. A man may cry out against sin of
> policy, but he cannot abhor it, but by virtue of a godly
> antipathy against it. I have heard many cry out against sin
> in the pulpit, who yet can abide it well enough in the heart,
> house, and conversation [life]. Joseph's mistress cried out
> with a loud voice, as if she had been very holy; but she
> would willingly, notwithstanding that, have committed
> uncleanness with him (Gen. 39:15). Some cry out against
> sin, even as the mother cries out against her child in her lap,
> when she calls it slut and naughty girl, and then falls to
> hugging and kissing it.
> TALK. You are trying to trap me, I perceive.
> FAITH. No, not I; I am only for setting things right. But
> what is the second thing whereby you would prove a
> revelation of a work of grace in the heart?
> TALK. Great knowledge of gospel mysteries.
> FAITH. This sign should have been first; but first or last, it
> is also false; for knowledge, great knowledge, may be
> obtained in the mysteries of the gospel, and yet no work of
> grace in the soul (1 Cor. 13). Indeed, if a man have all
> knowledge, he may yet be nothing, and so consequently be

---

[5] Original 'consider of one at once'.

no child of God. When Christ said: 'Do you know all these things?' and the disciples had answered: Yes; He adds: 'Blessed are you if you do them'. He does not lay the blessing in the knowing of them, but in the doing of them. For there is a knowledge that is not attended with doing: 'He that knows his master's will, and does it not'. A man may know like an angel, and yet be no Christian; therefore your sign of it is not true. Indeed, to know is a thing that pleases talkers and boasters; but to do is that which pleases God. Not that the heart can be good without knowledge; for without that the heart is naught. There is, therefore, knowledge and knowledge. Knowledge that rests in the bare speculation of things; and knowledge that is accompanied with the grace of faith and love; which puts a man upon doing even the will of God from the heart: the first of these will serve the talker; but without the other the true Christian is not content. 'Give me understanding, and I shall keep your law; indeed, I shall observe it with my whole heart' (Ps. 119:34).

At this stage, Talkative could see the writing on the wall: he was being shown up as one who could talk about spiritual matters, but knew nothing of them by felt experience. And it was embarrassing. And so he bridled.

TALK. You are trying to trap me again; this is not for edification.
FAITH. Well, if you please, propound another sign how this work of grace reveals itself where it is.
TALK. Not I, for I see we shall not agree.
FAITH. Well, if you will not, will you give me leave to do it?
TALK. You may use your liberty.
FAITH. A work of grace in the soul reveals itself, either to him that has it, or to bystanders. To him that has it thus: It gives him conviction of sin, especially of the defilement of his nature and the sin of unbelief (for the sake of which he is sure to be damned, if he does not find mercy at God's hand, by faith in Jesus Christ) (John 16:8; Rom. 7:24; John 16:9; Mark 16:16). This sight and sense of things works in him sorrow and shame for sin; he finds, moreover, revealed in him the Saviour of the world, and the absolute necessity of closing with him for life, at the which he finds hungerings and thirstings after him; to which hungerings,

etc., the promise is made (Ps. 38:18; Jer. 31:19; Gal. 2:16; Acts 4:12; Matt. 5:6; Rev. 21:6). Now, according to the strength or weakness of his faith in his Saviour, so is his joy and peace, so is his love to holiness, so are his desires to know him more, and also to serve him in this world. But though I say it reveals itself thus unto him, yet it is but seldom that he is able to conclude that this is a work of grace; because his corruptions now, and his abused reason, make his mind to misjudge in this matter;[6] therefore, in him that has this work, there is required a very sound judgment before he can, with steadiness, conclude that this is a work of grace. To others [than the man himself], it is thus revealed: 1. By an experimental confession of his faith in Christ (Rom. 10:10; Phil. 1:27; Matt. 5:19). 2. By a life answerable to that confession; *to wit*, a life of holiness; heart-holiness, family-holiness (if he has a family), and by conversation-holiness in the world; which, in the general, teaches him, inwardly, to abhor his sin, and himself for that, in secret; to suppress it in his family, and to promote holiness in the world; not by talk only, as a hypocrite or talkative person may do, but by a practical subjection, in faith and love, to the power of the word (John 14:15; Ps. 1:23; Job 42:5, 6; Ezek. 20:43). And now, sir, as to this brief description of the work of grace, and also the revelation of it, if you have anything to say by way of objection, object; if not, then give me leave to propound to you a second question.

TALK. No, my part is not now to object, but to hear; let me, therefore, have your second question.

FAITH. It is this: Do you experience this first part of this description of it? and does your life and conversation [that is, talk] testify the same? or stands your spirituality[7] in word or in tongue, and not in deed and truth? Pray, if you incline to answer me in this, say no more than you know the God above will say Amen to; and, also, nothing but what your conscience can justify you in; 'for, not he that commends himself is approved, but whom the Lord commends'. Besides, to say, I am thus, and thus, when my

---

[6] Bunyan was here edging into the puritan view of assurance, coupled with the common misunderstanding of 'the wretched man of Romans 7:14-25'. See my *Assurance*; *False*.

[7] Original 'professed Christianity'.

conversation [that is, way of life], and all my neighbours, tell me I lie, is great wickedness.

Here is the precise point: 'Do you experience this?' Ability to chat about the gospel, to talk about spiritual matters, is one thing, but the vital matter is the experience – the felt experience – of them. A man may talk about regeneration, he may be able to chat about it 'til the cows come home, but the question is: 'Is he born again?' And so on.

By this time, Talkative was finding the conversation too hot for comfort, and he could see fuel being added to the fire.

TALK. Then Talkative at first began to blush; but, recovering himself, thus he replied: You come now to experience, to conscience and God; and to appeal to him for justification of what is spoken. This kind of discourse I did not expect; nor am I disposed to give an answer to such questions, because I count not myself bound thereto, unless you take upon you to be a catechiser, and, though you should so do, yet I may refuse to make you my judge. But, I pray, will you tell me why you ask me such questions?

Faithful showed his courage by directly and personally confronting Talkative with the truth:

FAITH. Because I saw you forward to talk, and because I knew not that you had anything else but notion. Besides, to tell you all the truth, I have heard of you, that you are a man whose professed Christianity lies in talk, and that your conversation [that is, way of life] gives this your mouth-profession the lie. They say, you are a spot among Christians; and that professed Christianity fares the worse for your ungodly conversation [way of life]; that some already have stumbled at your wicked ways, and that more are in danger of being destroyed thereby; your professed Christianity, and an alehouse, and covetousness, and uncleanness, and swearing, and lying, and vain company keeping, *etc.*, will stand together. The proverb is true of you which is said of a whore, to wit, that she is a shame to all women; so are you a shame to all professors.

Talk about the last straw! Talkative had had more than enough. He was off:

TALK. Since you are ready to take up reports, and to judge so rashly as you do, I cannot but conclude you are some peevish or melancholy man, not fit to be discoursed with; and so adieu.

Bunyan drew the conclusion:

CHR. Then came up Christian, and said to his brother: 'I told you how it would happen; your words and his lusts could not agree; he had rather leave your company than reform his life. But he is gone, as I said; let him go, the loss is no man's but his own; he has saved us the trouble of going from him; for he, continuing (as I suppose he will do) as he is, he would have been but a blot in our company; besides, the apostle says: 'From such withdraw yourself'.

FAITH. But I am glad we had this little discourse with him; it may happen that he will think of it again; however, I have dealt plainly with him, and so am clear of his blood, if he perishes.

CHR. You did well to talk so plainly to him as you did; there is but little of this faithful dealing with men now-a-days, and that makes professed Christianity to stink so in the nostrils of many, as it does; for they are these talkative fools whose professed Christianity is only in word, and are debauched and vain in their conversation [way of life], that (being so much admitted into the fellowship of the godly) do puzzle the world, blemish Christianity, and grieve the sincere. I wish that all men would deal with such as you have done; then should they either be made more conformable to professed Christianity, or the company of saints would be too hot for them.

Then did Faithful say:

> *How Talkative at first lifts up his plumes!*
> *How bravely does he speak! How he presumes*
> *To drive down all before him! But so soon*
> *As Faithful talks of heart-work, like the moon*
> *That's past the full, into the wane he goes.*
> *And so will all, but he that HEART-WORK knows.*

May God deliver us all – I begin with myself – from mere talk. May we all have a felt-experience, a heart-experience, of Christ.

Appendix 2: Spurgeon on Power

Spurgeon, it goes without saying, made full use of the common expressions of Christendom, the institutional. Although I have written against this Christendom-speak,[1] in this Appendix I let most of Spurgeon's terms stand uncorrected since, as I have argued in the body of this work, Christendom, the institutional, is a major contemporary contributor to the practice I am critically addressing – outward show and talk, but no inward spiritual power or experience – and has been so this past 1700 years. Or, to put it another way, Christendom has encouraged outward show and chat at the expense of power; it has made a massive contribution to the replacement of reality with veneer. Indeed, the institutional cannot do anything other than produce the outward; it cannot produce inward power. The fact is, Christendom is absolute master of show and performance. And, as such, it is a disaster, conforming millions into a state of deception and delusion. If it is objected that countless men and women have savingly benefitted by the institutional, I respond by stating the obvious: God blesses despite – not because of – our practice. But God's blessing or otherwise does not warrant any disobedience to his plain word.

In 1889, Spurgeon, preaching 2 Timothy 3:5 in a sermon entitled 'The Form of Godliness Without the Power',[2] declared:

> They had a form of godliness. What is a form of godliness? It is, first of all, attention to the ordinances of professed Christianity... Every baptised person and every communicant at the Lord's table should be godly and gracious. But neither baptism nor the Lord's supper will secure this. Where there is not the life of God in the soul,

---

[1] See my *Public*, for instance.
[2] C.H.Spurgeon sermon number 2088.

neither holiness or godliness follow upon the ordinances. And thus we may have around us baptised worldlings and men who go from the table of the Lord to drink the cup of devils. It is sad that it should be so. Such persons are guilty of presumption, falsehood, sacrilege and blasphemy. Ah me, we sit beside such every time we meet![3]

The form of godliness involves attendance with the assemblies of God's people. Those who have professed Christ are accustomed to come together at certain times for worship and, in their assemblies, they join in common prayer and common praise. They listen to the testimony of God by his servants whom he calls to preach his word with power. They also associate together in church fellowship for purposes of mutual help and discipline...[4]

Christ's people are called sheep for one reason – they love to go in flocks. Dogs do very well separately but sheep do best in company. The sheep of Christ love to be together in the same pasture and to follow in a flock the footsteps of the good Shepherd. Those who constantly associate in worship, unite in church fellowship and work together for sacred purposes have the form of godliness and a very useful and proper form it is. Alas, it is of no value without the power of the Holy Spirit.

Some go further than public worship. They use a great deal of religious talk. They freely speak of the things of God in Christian company. They can defend the doctrines of Scripture, they can plead for its precepts and they can narrate the experience of a believer. They are fondest of talking of what is doing in the church – the tattle of the streets of Jerusalem is very pleasant to them. They flavour their speech with godly phrases when they are in company that will relish it. I do not censure them – on the contrary, I wish there were more of holy talk among professors. I wish we could revive the old habit: 'They that feared the Lord spoke often one to another'.

Holy conversation causes the heart to glow and gives to us a foretaste of the fellowship of the glorified. But there may

---

[3] Original 'every sabbath'. See my *Sabbath Questions*; *Sabbath Notes & Extracts*; *The Essential Sabbath*

[4] I am not so sure that this is common today.

be a savour of professed Christianity[5] about a man's conversation and yet it may be a borrowed flavour – like hot sauces used to disguise the staleness of ancient meat. That professed Christianity which comes from the lips outward but does not well up from the deep fountains of the heart is not that living water which will spring up unto eternal life. Tongue godliness is an abomination if the heart is destitute of divine grace.

More than this – some have a form of godliness upheld and published by religious activity. It is possible to be intensely active in the outside work of the church and yet to know nothing of spiritual power. One may be an excellent Sunday-school teacher after a fashion and yet have need to be taught what it is to be born again. One may be an eloquent preacher, or a diligent officer in the church of God and yet know nothing of the mysterious power of the Spirit of truth upon the heart. It is well to be like Martha in service. But one thing is needful – to sit at the Master's feet and learn as Mary did.[6]

When we have done all the work our position requires of us, we may only have displayed the form of godliness. Unless we hearken to our Lord and from his presence derive power, we shall be as a sounding brass and a tinkling cymbal. Brethren, I speak to myself and to each one of you in solemn earnestness. If much speaking, generous giving and constant occupation could win heaven, we might easily make sure of it. But more than these are needed. I speak to each one of you. And if I singled out anyone more than another to be the pointed object of my address, it would be the best among us – the one who is doing most for his Master and who, in his inmost soul, is thinking: 'That warning does not apply to me'.

My active and energetic brother, remember the word: 'Let him that thinks he stands take heed lest he fall'. If any of you dislike this searching sermon, your dislike proves how

---

[5] Original 'religion'. This note applies throughout Spurgeon's sermon.

[6] This, as so often, is hard on Martha. I recall a special preaching gathering where the world-famous preacher commended Mary at the expense of Martha, when all the while we all knew that within a few minutes we would be sitting down to a sumptuous tea – provided, no doubt, by the labours of several 'wretched' Marthas.

much you need it. He that is not willing to search himself should stand self-incriminated by that unwillingness to look at his affairs. If you are right, you will not object to be weighed in the balances. If you are, indeed, pure gold, you may still feel anxiety at the sight of the furnace but you will not be driven to anger at the prospect of the fire. Your prayer will always be: 'Search me, O God and know my heart: try me and know my thoughts: and see if there is any wicked way in me and lead me in the way everlasting'.

1 need not enlarge further. You all know what a form of godliness is and most of us who are here present hold fast that form – may we never dishonour it! I trust we are anxious to make that form accurate according to Scripture so that our form of godliness may be that into which the earliest saints were delivered. Let us be Christians of a high type, cast in our Lord's own mould. But do not become sticklers for the form and neglect the inner life – that will never do. Shall we fight about a man's clothes and allow the man, himself, to die?

But now, as these people had not the power of godliness, how did they come to hold the form of it? This needs several answers. Some come by the form of godliness in an hereditary way. Their ancestors were always godly people and they almost naturally take up with the profession of their fathers. This is common and where it is honest, it is most commendable. It is a great mercy when, instead of the fathers, shall be the children. And we may hopefully anticipate that our children will follow us in the things of God, if by example, instruction and prayer, we have sought it before the Lord.

We are unhappy if we do not see our children walking in God's truth. Yet the idea of birthright membership is an evil one and is as perilous as it is unscriptural. If children are taken into the church simply because of their earthly parentage, surely this is not consistent with that description of the sons of God which is found in the inspired Scripture – 'Which were born, not of blood, nor of the will of the flesh, nor of the will of man but of God'. Not generation, but REGENERATION, makes the Christian. You are not Christians because you can trace a line of fleshly descent throughout twenty generations of children of God.

You must, yourselves, be born again. For except a man is born from above, he cannot see the kingdom of God. Many, no doubt, lay hold naturally on the form of godliness because of family ties – this is poor work... grace does not run in the blood. If you have no better foundation for your professed Christianity than your earthly parentage, you are in a wretched case.

Others have accepted the form of godliness by the force of authority and influence.[7] They were, as lads, put apprentice to godly men. As girls, they were under the guidance of pious teachers. And as they grew up, they came under the influence of persons of superior intelligence and character who were on the Lord's side. This accounts for their form of godliness. Many persons are the creatures of their surroundings – professed Christianity or lack of it[8] is with them the result of circumstances. Such persons were led to make a profession of faith in Christ because others did so and friends encouraged them to do the same.

The deep searching of heart, which they ought to have exhibited, was slurred over and they were found among the people of God without having to knock for entrance at the wicket gate.[9] I do not wish anyone to condemn himself because he was guided to the Saviour by godly friends – far from it. But, nevertheless, there is danger lest we fail to have personal repentance and personal faith and are content to lean upon the opinions of others.

I have seen the form of godliness taken up on account of friendships. Many a time courtship and marriage have led to a formal religiousness, but a lacking heart. The future husband is induced to make a profession of Christianity[10] for the sake of gaining one who was a sincere Christian and

---

[7] Happily, I think this pressure is much less today than once it was in the UK. I recall trying to steer a conversation onto the spiritual when my wife and I met two wallers (men mending a stone wall) just outside a village in the Yorkshire Dales. I pointed to the large Congregational chapel close by, remarking on the number of people who must have attended at one time. One of the wallers, slowly straightening his back, replied to the effect that they had to, didn't they? Otherwise they would lose their job on the farm or in the woodyard or whatever. I could not deny the truth of it. End of conversation!

[8] Original 'irreligion'.

[9] Bunyan's *The Pilgrim's Progress*.

[10] Original 'religion'.

would not have broken her Lord's command (not) to be unequally yoked together with an unbeliever. Godliness should never be put on in order that we may put a wedding ring upon the finger – this is a sad abuse of profession of Christ.[11]

Other kinds of friendship, also, have led men and women to profess a faith they never had and to unite themselves outwardly or nominally with the church,[12] while in spirit and in truth they were never truly a part of it. I put these things to you that there may be a great searching of heart among us all and that we may candidly consider how we have come by our form of godliness. Certain persons assume the form of godliness from a natural religious disposition. Do not suppose that all unconverted people are without professed Christianity. Much religiousness is found in the heathen...

I mean, then, that to some the form of godliness commends itself because they have a natural leaning that way. They could not be happy unless they were attending where God is worshipped, or unless they were reckoned among the believers in Christ. They must play at professed Christianity even if they do not make it their life business. Let me remind you of the questionable value of that which springs out of fallen human nature. Assuredly it brings no one into the spiritual kingdom, for 'that which is born of the flesh is flesh'. Only 'that which is born of the Spirit is spirit'. 'You must be born again'. Beware of everything which springs up in the field without the sowing of the husbandman, for it will turn out to be a weed. O Sirs, the day will come when God will try us as with fire and that which comes of unregenerate nature will not stand the test but will be utterly consumed!

I do not doubt that, in these silken days, many have a form of godliness because of the respect it brings them. Time was when to be a Christian was to be reviled, if not to be imprisoned and, perhaps, burned at the stake. Hypocrites were fewer in those days for a profession cost too much. Yet, strange to say, there were some who played the Judas even in those times. Today professed Christianity walks

---

[11] Original 'religious profession'.

[12] Original 'unite themselves visibly with the church'.

forth in her velvet slippers.[13] And in certain classes and ranks, if men did not make some profession of Christianity,[14] they would be looked upon with suspicion and therefore men will take the name of Christian upon them and wear professed Christianity as a part of full dress.

The cross is at this day worn as a necklace. The cross as the instrument of our Saviour's shame and death is forgotten, and instead thereof, it is made the badge of honour, a jewel wherewith ungodly men may adorn themselves. Is this indicative of the deceitfulness of the age? Beware of seeking respect by a hypocritical godliness. Honour gained by a heartless profession is, in God's sight, the greatest disgrace. The actor may strut in his mimic royalty, but he must take off his crown and robes when the play is over. And what will he then be?

From the days of Iscariot until now, some have taken up the form of godliness to gain thereby. To make gain of godliness is to imitate the son of perdition. This is a perilous road and yet many risk their souls for the lucre which they find therein. Apparent zeal for God may really be zeal for gold...

Some love Christ because they carry his money bag for him. Beware of that kind of godliness which makes a man hesitate until he sees whether a duty will pay or not and then makes him eager because he sees it will answer his purpose.

Once more – I do not doubt that a form of godliness has come to many because it brings them ease of conscience and they are able, like the Pharisee, to thank God that they are not as other men are. Have they not been to church?... They can now go about their daily business without those stings of conscience which would come of neglecting the requirements of professed Christianity. These people profess to have been converted and they are numbered with believers. But, alas, they are not of them.

Of all people these are the hardest to reach and the least likely to be saved. They hide behind the defence[15] of a nominal professed Christianity. They are out of reach of the shot and shell of gospel rebukes. They fly among the

---

[13] Echoes of Bunyan's *The Pilgrim's Progress*.
[14] Original 'religion'.
[15] Original 'the earthworks'.

sinners and they have taken up their quarters among the saints. Sad is that man's plight who wears the name of life but has never been quickened by the Holy Spirit. Thus, I have very feebly tried to show what these men had and why they had it.

Let us now remember what they did not have. They had 'the form' of godliness. But they were denied 'the power'. What is that power? God himself is the power of godliness, The Holy Spirit is the life and force of it. Godliness is the power which brings a man to God and binds him to him. Godliness is that which creates repentance towards God and faith in him. Godliness is the result of a great change of heart in reference to God and his character. Godliness looks towards God and mourns its distance from him. Godliness hastens to draw near and rests not till it is at home with God.

Godliness makes a man like God. Godliness leads a man to love God and to serve God. It brings the fear of God before his eyes and the love of God into his heart. Godliness leads to consecration, to [progressive] sanctification, to concentration. The godly man seeks first the kingdom of God and his righteousness and expects other things to be added to him. Godliness makes a man commune with God and gives him a partnership with God in his glorious designs. And so it prepares him to dwell with God forever.

Many who have the form of godliness are strangers to this power and so are in professed Christianity worldly, in prayer mechanical, in public one thing and in private another. True godliness lies in spiritual power and they who are without this are dead while they live...

Look at the church of the present day... 'Having a form of godliness but denying the power thereof'. It is the sin of the age – the sin which is ruining the churches of our land...

May you be made of true metal! It were better for you that you had never been born than that you should make Christ dishonourable among the sons of men by leading them to conclude that professed Christianity is all a piece of acting.

The folly of this is illustrated by the fact that there is no value in such a dead form. The form of godliness without the power is not worth the trouble it takes to put it together and keep it together. Imitation jewels are pretty and brilliant. But if you take them to the jeweller he will give you nothing for them. There is a professed Christianity which is all paste gems – a godliness which glitters but is not gold. And in that day when you will want to realise something from it, you will be wretchedly disappointed...

There must be vitality and substantiality – or else the form is utterly worthless. And worse than worthless, for it may flatter you into deadly self-conceit...

Peter called hypocrites 'wells without water'...

My next is a word of discrimination. Those to whom my text has nothing to say will be the first to take it home to themselves. When I discharge my heart with a faithful sermon, certain trembling souls whom I would gladly comfort are sure to think that I mean them. A poor woman, in deep distress, comes to me, crying: 'Sir, I have no feeling'. Dear heart, she has ten times too much feeling. Another moans out: 'I am sure I am a hypocrite'. I never met with a hypocrite who thought himself one. And I never shall.

'Oh', said another: 'I feel condemned'. He that feels himself condemned may hope for pardon. If you are afraid of yourselves I am not afraid of you. If you tremble at God's word, you have one of the surest marks of God's elect. Those who fear that they are mistaken are seldom mistaken. If you search yourselves and allow the word of God to search you, it is well with you. The bankrupt trader fears to have his books examined. The sound man even pays an accountant to overhaul his affairs. Use discrimination and neither acquit nor condemn yourself without reason.

If the Spirit of God leads you to weep in secret for sin and to pray in secret for divine grace; if he leads you to seek after holiness; if he leads you to trust alone in Jesus, then you know the power of godliness and you have never denied it. You who cry: 'Oh, that I felt more of the power of the Holy Spirit, for I know that he could comfort and sanctify me and make me live the life of heaven on earth!', you are not aimed at either by the text or the sermon. For you have not denied the power. No, no, this text does not belong to you but to quite another class of people.

Let me give you a word of admonition. Learn from the text that there is something in godliness worth having. The 'form' of godliness is not all – there is a blessed 'power'. The Holy Spirit is that power and he can work in you to will and to do of God's good pleasure. Come to Jesus

Christ, dear souls. Do not come to the minister, nor to the
church, in the first place. But come to Jesus. Come and lay
yourselves at his feet and say: 'Lord, I will not be
comforted unless you comfort me'. Come and take
everything at first hand from your crucified Lord. Then
shall you know the power of godliness.

Beware of second-hand professed Christianity, it is never
worth the carrying home. Get your godliness direct from
heaven by the personal dealing of your own soul with your
Saviour. Profess only what you possess and rest only in that
which has been given you from above. Your heavenly life,
as yet, may be very feeble but the grain of mustard seed
will grow. You may be the least in Israel but that is better
than being the greatest in Babylon.

Four years earlier, Spurgeon, preaching on Hebrews 9:13-14,
in a sermon entitled 'The Purging of the Conscience',[16]
declared:

Without going into what the world calls actual sin, you and
I may come into contact with spiritual death; no, we carry
death about us, from which we daily cry to be delivered!
For instance, in prayer. Our prayer, in its form and fashion,
may be right enough, but if it lacks earnestness and
importunity, it will be a dead work. A sermon may be
orthodox and correct, but if it is devoid of that holy passion,
that divine inspiration without which sermons are but mere
pomp – it is a dead work! An alms given to the poor is good
as a work of humanity, but it will be only a dead work if a
desire to be seen of men is found at the bottom of it. Like
the almsgiving of the Pharisee, it will be a mockery of God!
Without a spiritual motive, the best work is dead! I confess
that I never appear before you without a fear that my
preaching may be a dead work among you. It must be so, as
it comes from myself – its life must depend upon the
spiritual power with which the Lord clothes it.

Do you not think that very much of common Christian
profession[17] is dead, or very near to it? You stand and sing,
but your hearts do not sing! You bow your heads in prayer,
but you are not praying! You read the Scripture, but it is not

---

[16] C.H.Spurgeon sermon number 1846.

[17] Original 'conversation'.

inspired to you, so as to breathe its own life into you! Even our meditations and thoughts about God's work may be mere intellectual exercises and so may be devoid of that power which, alone, can make them living works, fit for the service of the living God. Beloved friends, we need the precious blood of Christ to purge our consciences from this death and its working – and to lift us into holy and heavenly life! God is not the God of the dead, but of the living! God accepts not the dead sacrifice, but the living sacrifice. Even of old... the victim must be brought alive to the horns of the altar, or God could not receive it. We must not bring our dead faith or our dead words as an offering to God! Our prayers without emotion; our praises without gratitude; our testimonies without sincerity; our gifts without love – all these will be dead and, consequently, unacceptable. We must present a living sacrifice to the living God, or we cannot hope to be accepted – and for this reason we greatly need the blood of Christ to purge our conscience from dead works.

Do you not, sometimes, fear concerning your services that they have been altogether dead? When we are lukewarm, we hold the golden cup to our God, but he receives it not when our service is dead and chill. Indeed, he says of us when we are lukewarm: 'I will spue you out of my mouth'. The Lord cannot endure a worship which is half dead! All worship must be presented at blood heat – the warmth of life must be there. Do you not fear that even when, as a whole, it is alive, large parts of our service may be dead? Even in the living body of our prayers, may there not be a dead bone? Even in the living body of our praise, may there not be mortification in parts? God help us! What poor creatures we are! Is there one good thing about us? Are we not imperfect in our best works? Are not the sins of our holy things glaring before our consciences this day? Unless we are purged of this, by the blood of Christ, who offered up himself without spot to God, how can we serve this living God and be as priests and kings unto him?

In his *Flowers from a Puritan's Garden*, Spurgeon, quoting Thomas Manton: 'A corpse may be lavishly adorned – but there is no life within!', commented:

Adornments are out of place in the chamber of death – they do but make the scene the more ghastly!

We have heard of a dead prince who was placed upon a throne, dressed in imperial purple, crowned and sceptered! How pitiful the spectacle! The courtiers pressed to so wretched a travesty, must have loathed the pageantry!

So is it when a man's religion is a dead profession – its ostentatious zeal and ceremonious display are the grim trappings which make the death appear more manifest!...

It is not possible to supply the lack of the divine life. There is an essential difference between a dead child at its best – and a living child at its worst – and it needs no Solomon to see it!

Unless the Spirit of God... gives life, sustains life, and perfects life – none of us can ever dwell with the living God. This is the point to look to – the vestments and trappings are a secondary business.

'It is the Spirit who gives life; the flesh profits nothing!' (John 6:63).